THE POWER OF RELEASE

Transforming your life by breaking free
from limiting beliefs and achieving success.

SARA ZEIN

THE POWER OF RELEASE

Transforming your life by breaking free
from limiting beliefs and achieving success.

Content

Acknowledgments

I had always wanted to be a writer, a journalist, or a TV presenter. I believe that this is my call, and this is what I want to be. Even though I love one more than the other, they all seem very similar to me, belonging to the same field, and giving me the same feelings of joy and passion while doing any of them.

I would also like to be the successful doctor Ellen Pompeo in Grey's Anatomy or the powerful lawyer Gabriel Macht in Suits. The reason is not only the profession of a doctor or a lawyer itself, nor only because they do good stuff. It is beyond that. I might even like to be Alice Braga in Queen of South, who played the role of a powerful drug dealer. Yes, you read that right. While watching the series, I felt that I wanted to be her. Even though what she did was bad, she managed to succeed at it, becoming so damn powerful, and so out of reach. I loved how she went from nothing to sheer power and success.

That is who we are; we see success, we smell it, and we feel it. We love to embrace it. No matter what, we want it so badly because it is nice and it brings us money, power, fame, and all that we want. Or at least that is what we think.

To become successful, you might wait for luck to turn up, or you can decide to start working harder and smarter on yourself to achieve what you want. But before becoming successful in anything, you have to know what your thing is. Did you ever think "what is my thing?" What makes you alive is what's going to make you successful. But what is it? You might think you've already known it and earned it. But actually, you haven't, or else you'd already be successful by now having it all, or you might have it and still crave for more.

We're sharing the same mind and soul, and it is not only words you're reading, it is the reflection of yourself. That is the beginning of success, when you meet your true selfand get to know it better. That is the first step to real success.

I will walk you through some incidents in my journey, and I hope that you feel it and find yourself between the lines. So, you can reach the mindset I worked hard to achieve today. A place where life is a beautiful place, and success is a happy journey.

In this book, you'll learn how to know yourself first. You will know what you want to become. You will discover your real weaknesses and strengths and where you truly want to be. You will know what you want to become. Those discoveries, which you didn't know before, will tell you why you're not where you want to be yet.

After making sure of knowing your dream call, you'll pass through a lot to reach your goals.

You will let go of things and people that no longer serve you, and you'll make a room for new habits. You'll learn how to befriend and embrace your fears and utilize them for your own benefit, and you'll be more confident in yourself and jealousy will have no room in your world. You'll learn to love yourself and love serving and being kind to others. You will set your priorities in life, and most importantly, you'll maintain balance in everything, because balance is the only key to a successful and peaceful life. And after passing through all this, you will be ready for a happy, successful life.

Introduction

My name is Sara Zein. You can call me Sera, this is what people used to call me at work or on my social media accounts.

When I reached university, I was confused and didn't know what major I wanted to study. I felt lost, while most of my friends knew what they wanted since high school, or even before that. Maybe it was what they were told, and not their own choice. I never knew.

I did not know anything about my calling back then, and I did not notice that writing is my passion. I considered it as a hobby only, and I thought back then that I should study something that will bring me a lot of money. So I studied translation, but it wasn't my choice, it was my doctors' choice and they convinced me in a way. I didn't realize that nothing pays back more than doing what we love. Even if we don't make a big fortune, we'll be happy throughout the whole journey, and that is the most important thing. *Life will teach us that the journey is more important than the destination.*

It took me time to know what my calling is, and I studied a major for four years that I ended up not liking. Besides, I took a side job that occupied all of my time. I was paying for my university, so semester after semester, I found it hard to change my major and start over from the beginning. All I wanted is to graduate and be relieved from paying university checks. Despite that I love studying and learning new things and skills, but the checks were huge burdens on my shoulder.

In one of my summer semesters, I took a class named "Career and Life Skills" with Dr. Alissar El Shami. The course she gave helped in clearing my path and made me question myself a million times to know what I really wanted. And I'll give it to you now in my turn, hoping that I could help you save some time. Things that no told me about me back then and when I discovered them, it seemed too late to me. But it was never too late. Sometimes all you need is a wake-up call. All I want from writing you this book is to help you find yourself and find success and happiness in your journey, and to know what you want especially in your teenage years when you feel so confused and lost in choices, and no one helps you to discover your true self or guides you in your journey. Even people in their thirties and forties are still lost sometimes, and that is because they did not find the truth about themselves from an early age.

Some of us know what we want from our early school years, and we really go for it, and some of us stay confused about ourmessage in life till the age of 40 or above, and some come into this world and leave without even knowing what they really want, or what they really came for.

Each and everyone in this life should know that he or she is very important. They didn't come here by accident; they have a message they came to deliver before departing in peace.

It is very hard if you live as if you didn't exist at all. You spend all those years through their days and nights, through hard times and moments, through ups and downs. Everything around you falls apart, and you gather your broken pieces and manage to rise again. The cycle is repeated over and over until the end comes, and you go away without doing the right thing, leaving nothing behind to remind of you.

It doesn't have to look perfect, and it is not as simple as you might think. Knowing what you want and becoming successful isn't so easy or comfortable.

We think that if we know what we want, we will be confident all the time, and in complete control of our lives. But even the most successful and confident people have had some moments where they questioned what they were doing; if they were doing it correctly, and whether it was what they really wanted or not. But I can promise you that when you do like your choices, even if the road seems awful sometimes, you will be a happy person through the journey and this is a success. And I will walk you step by step, baby steps to live a happy, successful, and balanced life.

We all have many qualities and talents in us. And that's what chapter one speaks about; what is within you, what you are capable of, and who you really are.

Chapter one

Discover Your Power

*"The first secret of getting what you
want is knowing what you want."*

Learning Outcomes

Understand that positive self-esteem is essential to a successful career plan.

The 19 affirmations to build your self-esteem

Know about your eight types of intelligence

Understand the approaches and techniques necessary to develop a career success profile.

Know who you are and what you want

Build Self-esteem:

Self-esteem is our own evaluation of our worth. It is what we think about ourselves; it is the positive or negative thoughts we had about ourselves. We can build an empire with our self-esteem and we can crash one.

Your self-esteem starts to grow with you from an early age, you don't realize it but it is there from the beginning. What parents put in you is very important.

That's why there are good parents and bad ones. Parents are not those who feed you and put clothes on you only. They are those who feed your mind and make you feel that you matter. You are worthy.

When you grow up, you start realizing how it affects every aspect of your life, your appearance, age, financial difficulties, possessions, relationships, education, and family.

If you had a bad childhood where parents and teachers criticized you, it probably resulted in low self-esteem.

It is easy to know if you are that person with low self-esteem, you just have to focus on the way you treat yourself. If you say negative things to yourself when you do something wrong and become angry and frustrated for a long period, not forgiving yourself, then you have low self-esteem. Things can go wrong in this world; you just have to take it easy on yourself.

If your ex broke up with you and you went crazy and started calling and texting him while he didn't answer, you felt ashamed of yourself and it's normal. It might be wrong, but you don't have to live with the feeling that you are guilty, needy, and ashamed of yourself all the time. You have to forgive yourself. If you are that person, then you have low self-esteem.

If you think other people are better than you, that you are not worthy, and you always focus on your negatives, ignoring your achievements, you are that person, and you definitely need help.

This is a major problem and to fix you, we have to start with some tips that you should understand and work on daily, not just read them once in this book.

Start by saying these things out loud to yourself every day, and you will realize how your thoughts change and how positively they will affect your life from week two or three.

1. I am building positive self-esteem:

The ultimate goal is to like yourself. The more you appreciate yourself, the more likely you will get to achieve your personal and career goals. Our sources of self-esteem are deeply rooted; at a very young age, we begin to formulate a concept of ourselves based on our upbringing, schooling, culture, and our life experiences.

The goal and outcome of developing your career success profile will be to identify "You." You will clarify what makes you stand out so that your uniqueness becomes part of what others think of you and why others seek you out. Your brand, or reputation, reflects your philosophy, your values, and your consistent demonstration of who you are so that people in your personal and professional life know they can count on you for consistent performance. This reliability of character and action makes you a valuable and desirable asset.

2. I use positive self-talk:

Positive self-talk improves self-image. One of the most effective ways to improve your self-image is the deliberate use of positive self-talk. You already talk to yourself, and we all do constantly! But we usually are not consciously aware of our internal dialogues. Sometimes we are prone to self-defeating, negative messages that promote a poor self-image. Raising this internal dialogue to a conscious level can enable you to take charge of your self-talk. By repeating positive messages, you will haveapositive self-image. These messages are commonly called ***affirmations.***

You can create a new possibility. Remember, all events begin with a thought. If you think you can and believe that, then you can! Anything a person can conceive can be achieved.

3. I Visualize Success

Visualization, much like affirmation, is a mental practice. It is the conscious implanting of specific images in your mind. These images will become part of your unconscious and conscious mind through repetition, evoking and enhancing abilities, habits, and attitudes. Visualization differs slightly from affirmations because it involves specific *mental imagery* as opposed to *verbal expression* of positive thoughts. Indeed, visualization is referred to as mental imagery or mental rehearsal.

4. I Maintain a Positive Outlook

Do you have your definition of success? Regardless of the particular goals, you have in mind, you need to think positively to attain them. Have you ever heard the saying, "It's all in your head"? The people, who say this, believe our mental attitudes control our body and life and can therefore program our success or failure. Although many of our attitudes and beliefs come from early messages we received from our parents and teachers; as adults, we can choose to keep or change these messages depending on how helpful they are to us in achieving success and satisfaction in life. Examine your philosophy of life. *How you see life, in general, is how you lead your life.* A quick way to identify your philosophy is to examine how you visualize the future.

One may see life as:

A roller coaster, meaning that your life is beyond your control;

A mighty river to which you might adapt;

A great ocean with many directions and options;

Or just a game of chance

5. I am Enthusiastic:

You can become more enthusiastic about life by getting involved in something that has meaning for you. A hobby, volunteer work, mastery of a skill, or a new relationship all provide opportunities to generate and express enthusiasm. In your job, displaying a professional attitude includes acting as if things are fine even when you feel upset or depressed. Although it may seem phony, you will find that acting positively pays off.

6. I am Passionate:

Loving what you are doing and wanting to do it whether you are paid or not.

Passionate people understand their purpose.

7. I am Flexible:

Cultivate the ability to incorporate new information quickly and with ease into your current life, or emerge your career plan.

8. I have a sense of humor:

When you laugh, you are exercising all your internal organs. Learn to laugh at yourself. We would all benefit from lightening up a little and finding genuine humor in an embarrassing moment, in a mistake, or in a situation, that is so serious, that we end up laughing instead of crying.

Look for opportunities to see the lighter side of life and share the experience of being human with others who can laugh with you, not at you.

9. I am Assertive:

Being assertive means being the ultimate judge of our behaviors, feelings, and actions, and being responsible for the initiations and consequences of these actions.

Assertive personal traits include body language as well as words. Assertiveness is often associated with confident gestures rather than timid ones.

Positive assertive behavior shows that you have confidence in yourself.

10. I am Persistent:

Persistent people refuse to give up. They realize that accomplishing any goal takes time.

Success = passion and planning and persistence

The successful person is the one who keeps trying after not reaching a goal or after experiencing rejection, the one who keeps trying until his/her dream is attained.

11. I identify my goals:

Identified, written goals help move us to goal completion.

Most people don't reach their goals because they don't identify them. *If you don't know where you want to go, probably you won't get there.*

12. I initiate my action:

Successful people realize that goals activate people and fears stop people.

People who are afraid to tell the world what they want don't get what they want.

13. I have a vision:

For a balanced successful life, your vision needs to address as many aspects of your life as possible.

These include education, leisure, career, finances, health, relationships, personal and spiritual goals, and contributions to your community. *It is important to think big, even if you are not at all certain how you will get there.*

Share your vision with people you trust. You will encounter people who will offer you help to make it a reality.

14. I am innovative:

Innovation is discovering a new way to add value.

To think I could do this better is the seed of innovation, and you must not only think about how to improve it but step up and do it.

15. I am responsible:

Responsible people assume personal accountability for their lives. You realize you are in control of your thoughts, decisions, behaviors, and outcomes. You are self-reliant and action-oriented.

You avoid procrastination, recognizing that immediate action is the most efficient way to handle most situations.

Responsible people ask themselves always: "what's the best use of my time right now?"

16. I demonstrate emotional intelligence:

Emotional intelligence is the awareness and ability to monitor and control our emotions, thoughts, and feelings, and the ability to be sensitive to others.

The better you develop your EQ, the more successful you are likely to be.

IQ : gets you the job

EQ: keeps you employed and gets you promoted.

17. I am disciplined:

It is the ability to control or manage some aspects of your life, to have power over it.

Self-discipline is a vital component of success. If you lack the discipline to complete a task to accomplish your immediate goal, your long-term goals are less likely to be accomplished.

18. I am self-reliant and career resilient:

Successful employees need to demonstrate self-reliance and resilience.

These involve the ability to continually learn and develop new skills, initiate activities, demonstrate flexibility, and continuously align work with business needs.

19. I learn from role models:

We learn from and emulate others. If we consciously think about whom we admire and want to be like, we are more likely to begin thinking and acting in similar ways. We can choose our coaches and role models rather than simply being affected by the people who happen to be part of our current lives for better or worse. Think about the people you admire and begin to make a list. First, think globally about prominent individuals on the national and international scene. Then, think locally about people with whom you work; individuals who are part of your community, your neighborhood, or your religious affiliation; those who attend your school; or those who share your hobbies. Finally, think of the people who are dearest to you—your family and friends.

Which of their qualities do you admire? In what ways do you want to be more like them? Spend time observing them in action. You may want to consider telling them what you admire about them and asking them to tell you how they developed those qualities. Ask them for insights and suggestions that you might use to develop your success profile. Make these people part of your network of contacts. You will probably find that even the most successful people have struggled with moments of self-doubt or crisis of self-confidence. Ask them what they do when the going gets rough.

I'm not saying that you can be all of these points in one night, neither you can be all of them all the time. Take it easy. Read each point and how you can act to be it. Read it more than once, read it every day, and I promise you will begin to gain things that you were missing without realizing that. Because *what you feed your mind, becomes your mindset.*

And now I want you to test yourself and ask yourself many questions while reading this part because this is literally what makes me know that I love writing and I don't want anything more than writing in life. And that is what makes me happy today with what I'm doing. Because I knew what's my thing and I tried hard to be disciplined and work on each of the above points to become it, and I did it.

Every person has more than one intelligence. But you can't be successful in all areas. Your passion lies in one area more than the other. If you still don't know what's your passion, walk through each one of these types of intelligence and ask yourself where you feel that this is what makes you happy and passionate.

I have multiple intelligence:

- Eight distinct types of intelligence.

- Each person possesses all eight types of intelligence.

- Each intelligence can be more fully developed.

1. **Verbal/linguistic intelligence:**

   - Focuses on the use of language and words.

   - Interest in subjects such as English, foreign language, and history.

   - Interest in activities such as debate, drama, and yearbook editing.

   - Common career choices: *author, lawyer, teacher, salesperson, religious leader.*

2. **Musical/ rhythmic intelligence:**

   - Focuses on the ability to be aware of patterns of pitch, sound, rhythm, and timbre.

   - Interest in subjects such as music and dance.

   - Interest in activities such as band, orchestra, choir, and dance productions.

- Common career choices: *singer, composer, dancer, conductor, disc jockey, sound engineer.*

3. Logical/mathematical intelligence

- Focuses on the ability to think abstractly, problem-solve, and think critically.

- Interest in subjects such as math, science, economics, and computer programming.

- Interest in activities such as science projects, reading maps, spreadsheets, budgets, and blueprints.

- Common career choices: *engineer, scientist, mathematician, banker, economist, computer programmer.*

4. Visual/ spatial intelligence:

- Focuses on the ability to create mental images and transform them into art forms.

- Interest in subjects such as art, shop, drafting, and photography.

- Interest in activities such as designing brochures, ceramics, structures, and websites.

- Common career choices: *visual artist, designer, architect, webmaster.*

5. Bodily/ kinaesthetic intelligence

- Focuses on the ability to connect mind and body and relate to excelling at sports.

- Interest in subjects such as dance, drama, sports, and culinary arts.
- Common career choices: *athlete, coach, physical therapist, dancer, trainer, yoga instructor.*

6. **Intrapersonal intelligence:**

- Focuses on the ability to comprehend one's feelings.
- Interest in subjects such as psychology and creative writing.
- Interest in activities such as reading and journal writing.
- Common career choices: *psychologist, author, religious leader, career coach.*

7. **Interpersonal intelligence:**

- Focuses on the ability to comprehend others' feelings.
- Interest in subjects such as literature, psychology, and sociology.
- Common career choices: *counselor, psychologist, nurse, social worker, teacher, politician.*

8. **Naturalistic intelligence:**

- Focuses on understanding and working effectively in the natural world of plants and animals.
- Interest in subjects such as botany, zoology, and geology.

- Common career choices: *biologist, botanist, meteorologist, zoologist, veterinarian.*

We all have eight types of intelligence, but we have one more than the other. You might have three equally and feel you don't have the rest. However, you have them all but you're passionate about the first three; you feel they make you happy. To know and be sure what's your call, you have to practice and go further with each one because only experience and practice make you know for sure what you want.

Discovering what you want and what your call is, are the only chores that you get lost in time while doing because you do them out of passion, even though you are not getting paid.

Career success is based on a knowledge of self. The more you understand and accept your uniqueness and brand, the better you will be able to make appropriate life and career choices. Branding yourself for success is the first step of your assessment program.

Knowing yourself is very important just as knowing how to let go of things that no longer serve you.

This is what I will be talking about in chapter two.

Chapter two

Master the detachment

Just move on

Love is an intense feeling of deep affection. It is the most beautiful feeling in the world that makes us alive. It is the act of caring and giving to someone else. Giving pure feelings to someone is a big thing, and it makes you become a giver. You give without waiting for any return when you truly love someone. What makes them happy makes you happy. Their sadness is yours. You don't know why you love this person and when you ask yourself, you might not find any answer.

I used to have answers for why I love each person in my life. Until someone someday asked the man that I love why he loved me in front of me.

He answered: "Reason is powerless in the expression of love."

Rumi said, "Reason is powerless in the expression of love. Love alone is capable of revealing the truth of love and being a lover. The way of our prophets is the way of truth. If you want to live, die in love; die in love if you want to remain alive."

It can be for a family member, friends, colleagues, and even a stranger. You can love things too, books, words, and songs. Surrounding yourself with love will make your world a better place. *And the more love you put out there the more love you will get in return and in different ways.*

Loving someone is not different that much from love itself, but when you are in love you feel it stronger. Being in love makes you feel everything stronger and it even makes your soul feel free, but what happens when you lose this love?

The whole belief system in love changes in your life; you start questioning the concept and even your love for your family and friends, changes occur in your behavior, and you feel that you don't want anyone and you feel nothing for anyone, just because you have lost one person, the whole idea vanished to you. *Losing a thing or an important person makes us ungrateful for the other things and people we have because we focused all our emotions on our loss.*

We always look into the emptiness inside us; we always complain about what's missing, even though we know that nothing is perfect and we can't have it all. But we still do it. When we are in relationships, we want a single happy life, we don't want someone to tell us what to do, and what to wear. And when they are gone, we want that relationship and it finally seems perfect for us. But it's not. Because when we were in it, we complained a lot; we were not grateful, we did not thank the universe for what we had. We did not thank God either, and we always said out loud what we are missing and what we don't have. If you understand this, you'll know that half of the bad days and misery you're feeling after a breakup is because you're a victim of this mindset. You cry about what is missing and did not see what's there for you.

Maybe you'll read this chapter after months or years from the moment that I wrote it to you.

I passed through a very difficult time in the previous months because I was holding tight to a relationship that no longer exists in my life. I wasn't holding on to the person. I was holding on to my years and memories. Holding onto my history and my comfort zone. Holding onto a person who knows me the most. I didn't want things to end just because I didn't want to start all over again. I did not realize that everything has ended months ago.

You damage your spirit and soul when you hold onto a thing that no longer serves you. And you drag yourself down and the other person too.

I know I'm dead in this relationship and my soul is caged, but I do not dare end it. And whenever I feel a threat, I hold onto it more. I don't know why I was doing this, but the fear of letting go and regretting terrified me back then.

I was in this relationship for two years, maybe things were good in the beginning, but something turned off. But I tried not to admit it and lived as if everything is okay. I tried to end it sometimes, but when your partner is trying so hard, sometimes you keep going till they have the courage to end it. Or I did not want to end it, maybe because I didn't have the courage myself. I kept trying for months until I had Corona and it was hard; I slept for days, didn't call or see him, and after I felt better, I went to his place to find out that he was cheating on me.

I was shocked, I yelled, broke things, and cried. If you did see me that moment you will say she loved him a lot and he hurt her so badly. But no that wasn't the case. I did not cry for him or yell because of him. It's an egoistic reaction. That's how ego behaves so badly when it thinks that it lost the battle. I always say I hate ego; it only makes you suffer by giving afake alert.

When I left his house, *I left all my feelings, him and I, and all the memories in a footstep, they vanished while stepping out of his house.* Because there was nothing, we were nothing. I did not love him. I loved the way he used to love me. I loved the idea of being comfortable with someone who already knows what are my likes and dislikes.

I got to my car, and you might not believe me, but I was so relieved because I had those feelings deep inside that this relationship is not healthy and it was not going well. I was with a person who didn't deserve me, and there was something wrong about him that made me distrust him. I had a lot of red flags, but I did not look deep into them because I feared taking the decision.

Sometimes we confuse love with habit. And that costs us a lot. Time and energy are lost from a life that we'll only live once. And why? Because we did not know that we should not love someone toxic or someone who lets us down. Love is a better equation than this, love is freedom, its life itself. You do not love someone that does not deserve you. You only get along with those because of habit and the fear of losing something. *Even though losing sometimes is the best thing that will ever happen to you,* you did not know that.

Sometimes losing is your lucky strike. Steve Harvey said that sometimes God takes a better action than you because sometimes you are blind to see what's best for you. You don't dare to step outside, just because stepping outside means losing something. You did not learn to let go of what causes you pain, you did not learn that ending sometimes is the best beginning.

I thought that night about why we do this. Why do we ignore the signs and the feelings that something isn't right? Why do we stay when we must go? And why do we hold onto things when we must open the door and say goodbye?

I think we do this because we don't trust that we are powerful enough and that we can overcome anything, and we don't trust God enough in that he will take a thing and give another. He will close a door when a million doors will be open and waiting for us. We don't trust the universe and the idea of growing, changing, and adapting to new things. We don't trust evolution and Darwin's theory about species changing from year to year. There must be a change in our spirits and souls too. Not just in how we look and what haircut we got or what clothes we wear.

Today I'm so grateful for that loss because I'm alive and I'm with someone that makes me the happiest woman on earth. *If it wasn't lost, I wouldn't have gotten the gain I'm having today.*

Maybe God gave me my vision back that night after I had lost it for a long time. You may not think what I thought or be powerful as I was. You may have a difficult time after ending your relationship with someone you truly loved. I understand. But you have also to understand your worth. And whatever reason the relationship ended for or whatever that person left you for, they left you. They left you and abandoned your trust. They left you all alone. So now all you have is you. After you thought that you have someone who will always be there, he's not. And you go on from one relationship to another thinking every time that this is Mr. Right or Mrs. Right, but maybe they are not.

Every loss in life has a grieving process to pass through like when you lose someone and they pass away. When you face a career setback crisis, a friendship end, or a relationship breakup. But I'll focus here on the relationship breakup because this is what this chapter is about. But you can always use this as a technique in other things and in different ways, depending on the circumstances. Try at least to understand what you are feeling.

Relationship breakups pass through many stages, I will talk about the stages, but before that I want you to know that each stage could take you days, months, and maybe years. Only if you know your worth, you can make it faster and not waste your time on something that is only past and is just a memory now. *The Past is something that you no longer have the power to change. It's there far away, only in your head now. If you want to stay in it, stay. But you will be in a bubble that will explode anytime.*

The five stages of grief

It's called grief because when a relationship ends after loving someone, seeing them every day, talking to them, caring, sharing, having an intimate feeling, being there every day and all day for each other, and all of a sudden boom, NOTHING.

They are dead, no more calls, no checking, no morning massages nor good night ones. They are not there to stand by your side when you are sad anymore; they are not there to cheer you up. Also, they are not standing with the audience to clap for you, support you, and push you forward. They are gone. So, your soul wants to grieve over them, over the memories. So, you pass through those stages. But only you could decide how much time you want to grieve for your loss and waste your time.

The five stages of the grief model were developed by Elisabeth Kubler-Ross after she published her book on death and dying in 1969.

In her book, she makes it clear that stages are non-linear. People can experience these aspects of grief at different times and they do not happen in one particular order. You might not experience all of the stages, and you might find feelings are quite different with different bereavements.

Stage one

Denial

You feel lost. you don't accept what happened and you deny that the relationship has ended. Even if you know in your head that they are no longer here but you think that they may be back anytime, that they won't last without you, and that they will regret what they did. But sometimes they don't and they are gone. But hope is still there. It still gives you the energy to go out and look nice because in your head you think if they saw you happy, they will need to be part of your life again. But sometimes they no longer want to be in any part of your life.

Stage two

Anger

Days are passing, you're doing a lot without getting any response, no words, and nothing is cheering you up. They disappeared. They ghosted you. Nothing of your plan is making any progress in getting them back.

You feel that it's unfair, and you start getting angry, especially when you had a lot of plans with them that you didn't accomplish. You feel anger at them and you feel anger at yourself.

You blame yourself for things you did or things you did not do. You think if you behaved differently, you would have prevented that from happening.

Stage three

Bargaining

It's the "if only" or "what if" stage where you ask a lot of questions and repeat every single thing that happened. It is a stage in which you may try to negotiate with yourself or with a higher power to try to undo the loss. What if I did not yell? What if I did not wear the dress he doesn't like? What if, what if, etc. Your what-ifs are useless. Because even if you did whatever you did, I think there was a way to fix it if they wanted to.

Stage four

Depression

This is when you know they are not coming back.

This is the hardest stage when you feel that life no longer holds any meaning, which can be very scary. You feel sad, so sad and empty.

But you have to get sick before feeling well. So after the most dramatic moment you felt, you will become fine.

Stage five

Acceptance

Grief comes in waves and it can feel like nothing will ever be right again. But gradually most people find that pain eases, and it is possible to accept what has happened. You accept the fact that they are no longer by your side. You can learn to live again without them. My man taught me a lesson, whenever I feel sad about something he said, "think about it like a cigarette you burn in your hand. It's too painful in the beginning, you can't stop the pain, and it has to take the time needed to heal." And that what's your soul needs. Time to heal.

People you meet in your life, you don't make contracts with them to stay in your life to the very end, and you did not buy them or own them as your property. You also don't own them in any way.

When you meet someone new, you wish inside that they will be the perfect match for you, whether in business, friendships, or relationships. But that won't happen. Because you have to grow, you can't have the only friends you knew from your childhood and marry your best friend and work with your best friend and be the best partners. Some cases like those can happen but not always. You don't live thirty years to be only attached and glued to the first people you knew when you were four years old. This is not growth, not experience, and you will have no PR if you did that. You may have very few special people that stay by your side from the beginning to the end but not all of them will stay the same. *People grow and go in different directions. You can stick around and wait and live on memories, and they will pass over you. And you will be there hanging with your memories.*

There are three kinds of people. People who enter your life just for a reason, and most of the time you don't see the reason at the moment but you see it later and feel it. It may be a big lesson and it might be the very small things that they let you see, feel or know.

I have a friend named Amal Taleb, that once told me, "Sara I stayed with him for a year, I did not see why I spent with him 365 days. Nothing positive happened, not a single thing that I learned. Nothing at all. But after years, I was sad in my car and I put on a song that changed my whole mood that day. And that song was a song I would never know about if he didn't make me hear it because it's not famous and no one knows it. So that day I realized that the whole year's benefit was only that song. But that song resulted in something good after years."

Even the little things that don't matter to you at that moment make sense after a while. Just be patient.

The second kind of people are those who come along for a season and those are the most people we meet. Because deep inside we are all seasonal people. We don't know it, but we are.

We feel we are down in some period in our lives, so we search for people who are funny and go out a lot and we start partying with them every night. But this is not our nature, we don't party a lot. If we do, we won't discover that we love partying at the age of thirty-six or forty. We would know it before. But it's just a phase.

Or we feel that our life is empty and boring, and we know someone who plays tennis, so we start going with them every day, not because tennis is our hobby but because we might like it and it may become a hobby, and we started it because we want something new. So, it's not wrong to be a seasonal person in someone's life or to have a seasonal person in your life because you teach each other something.

Life is about giving and receiving; the more you give, the more you take. I don't see that kind of people as bad people because I think we all need to take or have small things that light our life a little or take us in different directions sometimes, and we could find it in those people.

And the third kind of people are the lifetime people; those who stay with you all along, and they are very few. They clap for you when you did it and cry for your loss when you lose. They watch you grow and go in many different directions. They watch you all the time and are by your side. Those are the people that you must choose carefully.

If you become aware of the three kinds of people and you understand that it's sometimes for your benefit, you won't feel sad about every person that leaves your life. Instead, you will be happy and know that the closed door will open a new opportunity and experience. So why won't we grow and expand our roots? So, one day we will know what we are and what people we want and need in our life.

Once a wise man told me, "I categorize every person in my life, even my family members. I have people for fun. I go party with them, but I don't take them seriously, work with them, do business with them, or cry on their shoulders. I want them just when I want fun. I have people whom I trust, they are the keepers, I come to them when I need advice or when I have a big thing, and I lean on them. But I don't go crazy around them. And so on." He categorizes every person and he's so happy. He thinks every person has a thing and he takes the best from everyone. And he can easily adapt to the idea of anyone disappearing. He did not do and enjoy everything with one single person because if that person leaves, everything falls. But what if you do everything with the same person and you lose him?

Try to take care of people who make themselves a world full of everything for you. But if they want to leave, don't try to cage them. They might give you the best things and now it's your time to give to someone else.

I know it's hard when it comes to love, to a partner whom you adore and have feelings for. You can't stand waiting for them and you can't help yourself get over them as they do.

But some people hurt you badly, and those people don't deserve your time and energy. They don't deserve to grieve over them even. All you have to do is to know your worth and make your time important to you.

They don't deserve to be buried even. Just move your leg a step forward over their dead bodies and that's it!

Now you are free to walk, run, or fly.

Whatever way suits you to continue your life, just do it.

Some people are powerful enough to try after a very harmful breakup.

They do their best and accomplish a great achievement after this.

Others walk slowly in baby steps to adapt to the new life after this.

Both are good, there isn't a wrong way.

There is who you are and what your personality is and how you know to manage your life in the best way that suits you.

You can walk baby steps till the end of the tunnel where you meet the light.

And you can fly over the tunnel if you learned how to truly love yourself and love what's best for you.

I will give you my philosophy about the eleven days that I think are enough for you to grieve over someone that doesn't deserve grief. Because they don't bother for a second thinking about you. So, hell, eleven days are too much even for them.

But these steps are just if you are one hundred percent sure that this person did not love you and won't be back.

I'm not going to lie to you. In my relationships, I love to take my time to respect what was between me and the person if they deserve my respect, and I'm not with the idea of forgetting the person you loved the second day if he's a good person. Only you can know what you're dealing with. And only you can feel if he betrayed you, or did not love you, or if he's not that bad and it's God's will, not meant to be.

You will pass over the five stages of grieving in those eleven days. But you will help yourself overcome it if you do this.

Day one to Day three: it's the phase when you still didn't find the solution or how to help yourself. You are still stuck somewhere where you can't believe what happened and you think deep inside that the person who abandoned you will return and regret their decisions. And you will wake up tomorrow and nothing of this will be true. But you wake up tomorrow and they are gone. They are no longer there in your days, they don't send a good morning message and not a goodnight one, and they are not here to make you calm when you are sad. They can't help you solve your problems because they no longer care about your problems. They are gone, they might be starting a new life already and interested in someone else already while you are suffering.

This phase we might call denying. As I talked about it earlier, denying is the phase where you think that they will be back. And you're not believing that this is happening.

I'm not with distracting yourself when you lose someone, that is not healthy, it's like ignoring our feelings, and *our feelings need a home to feel safe and express what they are going through.* So, we have to give them time.

I think denying the case and being angry about the situation could take three days maximum. You can do nothing more than sit in your bed. Crying, missing them, repeating what happened, questioning yourself, and then getting angry with yourself and them.

Day four to Day six: After three days you still feel frustrated, nothing changes, and you still miss them. In this case, I suggest you pass through all your history together. Look at all your pictures and read all your chats together if needed. And then write them a letter. A letter that they won't read. A letter from the heart to the heart. Write everything you feel. How you missed them. Beg them if needed. But don't send it.

Make a fire night, drink some wine, and burn all their stuff. Delete all your chats with them and all the pictures you have for them.

After six days of crying, shouting, breaking things, and burning other things, it's time to think logically, right?

Day seven and eight: They left you! No matter what you are going through, they are not coming back. So, it's time to find a solution and look at your miserable self.

Put a paper, list their good and bad qualities, and the qualities you want and need in a relationship. See if they match them. I don't think they do. Because I don't think the qualities you want are in someone who abandoned you! See the balance between their advantages and disadvantages. And then I think you will find that something was missing from the beginning. Something that you were not seeing.

In the last three days, I think you should not be liking the situation they put you through, and youwant to get out of it. Because the point of feeling sad and not distracting yourself will make you see clearly that they hurt you a lot to let them go. That's why I'm not with the idea of distracting ourselves because when we are distracted, we might disrespect ourselves and be distracted from the pain they gave us and miss or text them. That's why I think it's so healthy to be alone for eleven days and live the grief. And usually, people who distract themselves stay longer in love with the people that abandoned them, while people who live their grief and express their feelings forget more easily. So, these days are the ones after burying everything that belongs to them or reminds you of them.

You should be searching for things to get you back to whom you were before meeting them. You were a funny person. Weren't you? You were confident. You loved yourself. Why should you let someone take all the good qualities you have with them? Try to gain them back. Step by step. Start thinking that you lived without them for long years before they came along. And you were good. Stop imagining your life with them and how it is hard without them.

Be grateful for what you have, in a moment of loss we forget all the good things that God gave us. We forget our good parents, our good friends, the nice car, the hobby we enjoy, the love of food, and the good taste of it. We forgot our eyes and how we can see the sunset and the sunrise. We forget every nice thing and only look at the ones we missed. So, Start being grateful for what you have, and believe in God and the universe that when something is gone it's for our good. Better is coming.

And on the tenth night before going to bed promise yourself that tomorrow is a better day. And the sun will rise again and that's enough to assure you that there's a better tomorrow. I can't promise you that you will be forgetting them and they will be gone. But you can now start distracting yourself with life and time will heal your pain. Only after you express your feelings and feel the pain you can be fine and be okay and live again.

On the morning of the eleventh day, wake up early. Look at your reflection in the mirror and tell yourself that you love it so much, you deserve to be happy, and you won't let yourself down anymore. Take a shower, and clean your soul from negative vibes, not only your body. Inhale happiness and hope, exhale sadness and pain. Dress nicely and go out and face the world for the new journey.

The good thing is that God created us to forget the good long talks and the nice stuff that our partner did to us when the relationship ended and they ended it in a bad way. The only thing we kept remembering and replying to is how they left us and the way they did it. And this makes us stronger. Because you can't forget someone if you kept thinking about their kindness and nice supportive words.

Maybe one day when it's all gone, you will remember the nice moments as memories in your journey, and you'll laugh at the end.

Only time will tell.

Letting go of toxic relationships and situations that no longer serve us is a powerful step towards gaining confidence and self-respect. By prioritizing our own well-being and creating healthy boundaries, we can cultivate the inner strength to pursue our goals and build fulfilling relationships based on mutual respect and support.

So, the next chapter will be about how to regain your confidence if you lost it, and how to gain it if you don't have it.

Chapter three
Wear Confidence

The moment you doubt it, you lost it

What is confidence?

Confidence comes from within, from your feelings about yourself, acceptance of your body and mind, and belief in yourself and your abilities, skills, and experience. It's to have a sense of control in your life.

It comes from being grounded in your sense of self, remembering who you are and what you value, and what hard work you've put in.

A confident person does what he wants in the way he wants. Even if he does something for the first time, he is not afraid to be the first who did it. Because confident people put their own touch on the things they do, they are willing to take risks without caring or fearing others' opinions. Not everyone is born with this, but the good thing is that you can earn it.

On the other hand, low self-confidence might make you feel full of self-doubt, passive or submissive, or have difficulty trusting others. You may feel inferior, unloved, or sensitive to criticism. Feeling confident in yourself might depend on the situation. For instance, you can feel very confident in some areas, such as academics, but lack confidence in others, like relationships. Sometimes it can be hard to develop confidence, either because personal experiences have caused you to lose confidence or because you suffer from low self-esteem.

Low self-confidence might stem from different experiences, such as growing up in an unsupportive and critical environment, being separated from your friends or family for the first time, judging yourself too harshly, or being afraid of failure.

Having high or low self-confidence is rarely related to your actual abilities, and is mostly based on your perceptions. Perceptions are the way you think about yourself and these thoughts can be flawed.

Why should you work on your confidence and why is it very important?

Confidence is one of the most qualities that you should work on to earn in your life because it attracts people and makes them want to invest in you in business or be around you in life.

It gives people positive energy around you and makes them trust you and trust your words. When you are confident about yourself or about any subject you are talking about, you make others listen and become convinced.

You might be confident in some areas more than others. It depends on your strength and information and how you master things you talk about and act about.

Imagine that you don't have any confidence in any area. What would your life look like?

You go out there, always feeling less than anyone, and you are always quiet, afraid to speak up or to say your opinion out loud because someone might make fun of you. It is not because your opinion is bad, in the end, it's your opinion, but you don't dare to say it out loud. You don't see that it matters, you don't feel that you matter. However, in this world when you don't say what you want and act on it, you don't reach what you want.

If you are too shy and feel down anddepressed because of anyone's negative opinion or criticism towards you, then how could you survive and have good days?

How could you work on what you want and be the best if you don't even have a voice to speak up?

It started from the day you were at school and did not read that paragraph out loud because you don't want anyone to laugh. You start postponing it and this continues till today, trying to be in the shadow so no one notices you.

The biggest part that makes you gain confidence is making mistakes and doing better next time. It's learning and taking risks, trying things you know nothing about but having the courage to try and learn from.

You do not have to do everything in life perfectly, but you have to be open to try and explore yourself to know yourself better.

Nowadays, on social media (Instagram and TikTok), I have seen a lot of people with dumb stuff; they are so silly. They can show you their beauty, but they are not smart enough to have a decent and meaningful conversation. They look just like a painting in a museum but are not even that artistic and deep, and despite that, they dare to be out and loud, whileyou are still thinking if you could do it.

Look at them. They are going viral because of very silly and substandard videos and live streaming and gaining a lot of money. I'm not saying that all of them don't deserve to be known. Some of them deserve it, at least they drew a smile on your face. But some don't. But I'm not the kind of person that will watch others and criticize them. I clap for those who did something out of nothing. The world is always ready to give you opportunities if you are ready to accept them. So, I encourage anyone to show who they are, what they want, and what they are made of.

I know what type of people I'm speaking about exactly, shallow people who have nothing to show except their bodies, or only need to be vulgar and cheap to go viral. Thus, we live in a silly world, and the people who are following these kinds of people are even sillier than them. So, if you think you are more worthy, then it's your time to go out and speak out loud!

We need you. We need people with minds. Don't let silly people put you down, and don't give them power over your mind.

Try to gain some confidence to step up and take over to create a better world and a more intellectual generation.

You can have your place in the world, and they can have their own. You are not competing with them, but you should have the good that some people are waiting for. Some people need to see the good to know the bad.

It's normal to feel shy or to panic sometimes when you want to speak in front of a lot of people. You can have a presentation in front of a small group of friends for example. It's a normal feeling, that you may have, which doesn't mean that you are any less confident.

When you share your opinion out loud or your knowledge with different minds and cultures, some will love you and some won't, and this is a part of life. Not everyone has to agree with you to be great and to feel that you can do it.

I'm not saying that I'm always confident and in my best shape; I'm one of you and like you. But I always help myself when I feel down. I always remind myself of who I am and what I'm capable of and I act on it. So I can regain my confidence when it is lost in day-to-day problems and difficulties.

The good news is that you can gain confidence if you start practicing some of the techniques I'll give you.

First of all, I want you to believe in yourself, to have faith in yourself and faith in God, and that you are always in good hands no matter the obstacles that you are facing.

Believe that you are powerful, beautiful, and smart.

Start recalling these words every time you are free and whenever you feel down, and replace the negative thoughts with positive ones. Start saying that you can and you will and that you believe in yourself and God. Then, you'll see the magic of how this will work after a short period.

I remember a friend of mine who was so beautiful, and she met a man, who was a lawyer, and they started dating. She told me that whenever she was out with him, she felt uncomfortable. She felt that she was always in a state of fear that he might speak about things she doesn't understand or doesn't have any idea or opinion about.

She always felt so shy when he introduced her to one of his friends, and they asked her about what she does in life.

She did nothing.

She mostly feared the question: "tell me about you."

She feared when they used English words a lot, and she didn't comprehend some terms, or when they said an inside joke and they laughed, while she did not have the slightest idea about it.

She loved him, but she felt she wanted to end the relationship. When I asked her why, she said that he considers himself the man that knows everything, and he's arrogant. I asked her why she felt this way, and she told me about some of the things that happened during the relationship.

I realized that he is a smart man with a lot of knowledge about many things. He reads a lot; he made himself smart and confident, and she wanted to run away from him because he's better than her. Because when he's around, she felt that she's nothing and that her opinion doesn't matter if she even had one.

So, the problem wasn't him, it was her. However, the biggest problem was that she did not realize that she has to have an education, have her own career, likes, and dislikes, have some hobbies, read and have general knowledge about some topics, have value, and be somebody.

But it's normal to feel what she felt, and it's not wrong. It's healthy. It's great to be around people who are smarter than us, this will make us challenge ourselves to be better. No matter how much we feel weak or even stupid around some people, we should work on ourselves to be stronger and know more. Its good to know that we lack something, and what is right is that we have to work on educating ourselves, not hiding or running away from those people that challenge us. That was her mistake.

To be something and to be respected on the table you're sitting on can only be achieved by you. It's you who can make a man respect you and become interested in your opinions and thoughts. It's you who can make people want to know what you think and what you want to say.

If you have nothing to do, why bother yourself and live?

I started giving her some tips to help her grow and be a better person, things that she must work on, not for him, but for herself, her life, her mind, her spirit, and her future.

You can also use these tips to regain your confidence back or to have one if you don't.

Start with the basics: shower, take care of your smell, nails, and hair, wear nice clothes, and always buy some new ones to feel up-to-date and beautiful. Of course, you should be happy and confident about how you look, and I do not underrate taking care of your physical appearance, but this can be achieved easily. However, it is not everything, and it should not define who you are.

Start by achieving small things

Did you hear about the bucket list and its importance?

The most famous and richest people in the world start by writing everything down as a bucket list or on a board that they can see every day. Starting to accomplish little things will give you the confidence to feel that you can achieve bigger things. Do a list of things you would like to accomplish and start ticking off each thing you did.

Pause reading the book now and get paper and a pen, write your bucket list, and write every single thing you love to have or try at least once in life. Don't make your list less than a hundred things or you would be limiting yourself otherwise. Put whatever comes to your mind; life is full of many different areas, no way you could have less than one hundred things that you love to try once at least.

Set some goals

even if they are small goals, and begin with small ones so that one day you can accomplish big achievements. That will help you accomplish big dreams because it gives you a great feeling about yourself and that you're doing great. It also makes you more confident.

You can begin with day-to-day goals, and what you need to accomplish today, this week, and this month.

If you accomplish the goals you set for every day, chances are you will begin meeting weekly and monthly goals.

Big changes do not happen overnight.

If you want to have a good shape, start by going to the gym twice a week at least. That will make you want to achieve the perfect body you want. If you want to have more knowledge about a specific subject, you can start by reading a book in a one-month timeline about this subject. Or if you want to be close to your family and be around them if someone needed you, spend some time with your family. Monitoring is the best way to know if you're making progress. Write down whatever your goal may be. It will help you stay on course, and you will build confidence as you see the progress you're making in real-time.

Do more of what makes you happy

Get a hobby

You can always find something that makes you happy. something that you're passionate about and you have time for it. It could be photography, sports, writing, reading, cooking, or anything else! When you've worked out your passion, commit to giving it a go. Chances are, if you're interested or passionate about a certain activity, you're more likely to be motivated and you'll build skills more quickly. Create space for it because life is short; you need time to enrich your life and to recharge to be your best self.

Think of things you are good at.

Everyone has strengths and talents; think about things that you are good at. That gives you a good feeling about yourself, and feeling good about yourself is very important to build confidence. Ask yourself what you are good at and try to build on those things. Maybe you could start doing these things more often because they will help you boost your confidence. If you like dancing, start taking dancing classes; if you like painting and you think you are good at it, start doing it.

Don't you ever say that you don't have time for your hobbies; you got 24 hours every day, and you can always make time even if you start with giving little time for things that you love, so it becomes a habit and after a while, you will start feeling that you can't live without doing those things. Because they give you nice feelings, you will feel alive when you do what you like the most. And that will make you feel happier and happiness leads to more confidence.

Do the right thing, not the easiest

We all procrastinate, who does not do this? We always postpone things that we have time for till later just because it's hard or needs effort, and the more we did that, the more we are late in reaching where we want.

Stop making excuses for not doing the right thing, it's all in your head.

Most confident people live by a value system and make their decisions based on that value system, even when it's hard and not necessarily in their best interest, but in the interest of the greater good. Your actions and your decisions define your character. Ask yourself what the best version of yourself that you aspire to be would do, and do it. Even when it's really hard and it's the last thing you want to do and it means a short-term sacrifice on your part, in the long run, you're going to like yourself more and be prouder of who you are.

Be fearless

Failing isn't your enemy, it's fearing failure that truly cripples you. If you set big goals and have big dreams, you're going to feel overwhelmed, and you're inevitably going to feel like you can't do it. In those moments you have to look inside yourself, gather every ounce of courage you have, and just keep going. I don't see fear as a bad thing in every situation. It's good sometimes to be afraid of things, it makes you stronger and I'll talk about this later. *Every single wildly successful person has been afraid, and they've kept working and taking risks anyway because what they are trying to accomplish is more important and urgent than the fear of failure.* Think about how much you want to achieve your goal, then put your fear to the side, and keep going, one day at a time.

Most of the time you feel that you have an incredible idea and some let you down. They made you feel that your idea is so stupid and it might not work, and after a while, you hear of someone who became successful in something you were thinking about. Not because they have much more skills than you have to do it, but because they know that even if they are afraid of failure, they might take risks sometimes and believe in themselves.

People change the world every day, despite everyone around them telling them it can't be done. If you think you can do it, you can. Don't listen to them, believe in yourself, and keep going.

You should not let fear stop you from dreaming big.

There's a great line in *10 Things I Hate About You* when Joseph Gordon-Levitt is about to give up his pursuit of Larisa Oleynik, and Heath Ledger gives him a pep talk, ending it with, *"Don't let anyone, ever make you feel like you don't deserve what you want."*

Think positive

This is the most important to me. I tried everything in my life and if I missed this one, nothing went right. For example, you can't prepare and study for an exam very well, when all you're thinking about is that you're not going to pass. You won't pass then.

You have to think positively, imagine good things, and talk about yourself in a good way. That's why I told you self-esteem is a very important thing because it's all connected, you have to have a little at least from everything. You can't feel confident if your self-esteem is very low and if you don't respect yourself and know your worth.

Every one of us has times when we feel we are not good enough, but we should always remind ourselves of the positive things that we have.

It's easy to lose your confidence if you always remind yourself that you had not accomplished any good things in your life. That will make you feel that you are such a loser, so you should always remind yourself of the good things and goals that you have achieved.

Make a list of things you are proud you did in life, like graduating, taking a French class, learning how to dance, practicing yoga, or opening a small business or a big one. Whenever you feel down, grab this list and remind yourself that a bad day or week doesn't mean that you did not accomplish anything in your life.

Treat yourself like you would treat your best friend and cheer yourself up. Positive talk and energy make you a better person surrounded by good vibes that help you think and be better.

Exercise

Exercise is good for your health in general, it's good for your heart, lowers blood pressure, prevents diabetes, helps you lose weight, helps manage stress, and prevents depression. It increases the production of endorphins and leads to an increase in feel-good chemicals, such as serotonin and dopamine.

It also boosts attention, memory, and comprehension.

Exercising makes your day feel active, your energy aroused, and it affects your mood also.

So, start today.

Fake it until you make it

Maybe you don't own any of these qualities above, but you should try and start owning them. While starting this and until it makes you feel that you earn this confidence, I suggest you fake it until you make it.

It is an English aphorism that suggests that by imitating confidence, competence, and an optimistic mindset, a person can realize those qualities in their life and achieve the results they seek.

I don't usually like faking things, but I watched it happen.

Years ago, when I was still in college I worked with a beginner wedding planner, I don't want to say his name because he's very famous nowadays. He might not like me to give an example of him that he faked it in the beginning, but he did. Back then, he could only plan some very small weddings, but he had pictures and videos for big weddings, and no one imagined that he could do it one day.

When he used to gain only two hundred dollars from a whole wedding and show the groom and the bride weddings outside the country with huge installations and designs that he had no idea about even and were worth millions, I laughed.

But after about 5 years only, he did it. He did the biggest weddings all over the world, and he transformed from Mr. no body to the number one wedding planner with a private jet.

So, this is what fake it until you make it can do.

It's all in your head, if you want to work on a thing that you think you lack, you can do it. Step by step. Just don't give up on yourself because you deserve a million shots.

Confidence may be lost, if you overwhelm yourself. Always focus on things that matter to you, and this is what I'll be talking about in chapter four

The Art of Freedom

When you want to fly, throw the burdens on your way up

We live in a life where there are a lot of things that might happen any second that we don't see coming. Your sister wants to divorce; a family member is so sick, your parents are broke, your best friend caught her fiancé cheating, and she is crying and shouting and in need of you, your car tires are destroyed because of a big pit in the road on your way to an important meeting. Yet, this is all only minor. Major things may happen in the country you live in, a huge fire, an explosion, war, no electricity for days, flood, and I don't know what else could happen.

I can't tell you any of this is not going to happen, and I can't tell you that there's a way that won't make you feel that it's too much or that you can't handle any of this. Also, I can't guarantee that I can handle it all and be happy all the time. I struggle sometimes with these things. I'm not here to lie or tell you bits of bits of advice that we can't do. But I'm going to assure you that we will try. We will understand the concept and try to work it out.

There are a lot of videos nowadays that give you solutions for everything you are suffering from in less than one minute, but this is not going to work. You don't have to trust someone that tells you there is such a thing in this world called magic and that a simple word can change your whole world. It's a lie. I can't change your world with a word and no one can either. But I can work with you through the concept that you find logical, and you are convinced by and try to work on it day by day till your problems are solved, then you can say this word or video changed my life. But actually, it doesn't in one moment, it takes time, energy, and discipline to reach the point where you want to be.

While writing this chapter my friend decided to divorce and I was too busy with my work and studies that I felt that it was not the right time and that I can't give her all the time and care she needed because I have a lot to do. That stressed me a little bit, but I always repeat and remind myself of this incident and any other when I feel I lack it and need to be in shape.

So don't feel that you have to be powerful and always at peace; sometimes on the way, you lose it.

This chapter will teach you to take care of things that only matter and worry about the only things that will add to your life. So, you can save time and energy.

It's not a magic trick, some things become fixed just when you understand the concept and understand your mindset and how to shift it.

Maybe it sounds difficult at first, but when you master it you will find that this is one important key to true happiness that lasts more than you imagine. Because after knowing how to deal with this, you don't have to worry anymore about things that are not important to you or about things that you can't control at all. It's all about saving the most beautiful energy for the best moments, to work hard for the true value of your life. Before I mastered this art, I admit that I wasted a lot of time worrying about what others thought, what they said, who is sad, and how to fix everything around me, but it is impossible to fix or control everything. It's a waste of energy, so you should instead take good care of what matters to you and makes you happy.

It's nice to help and very nice to serve others but you don't have to lose your power and energy for others who have a lot of negativity and will drag you down on their way.

We all have our problems, so try to help because you are here to help and servekind heartedly.but don't let any problem in the world be your problem. You will feel down and when you are down you can't serve anyone or help your beloved ones. So save some energy.

I just want to pause here and ask you a question. Because as I said I'm not here to give you advice, I'm here to tell you things no one told me before when I was younger. I wish I can help some of you to understand how to think in the right way because no one is coming to save you from your mindset, there's no magic, this is a lie. You are the only magic you got, and sometimes, only God can help you and change your situation.

My question is: Do you believe in God? In Destiny?

If you believe in those things, you should know that there are things that you cannot do anything about when it happens. Things that you have no control over, sometimes all you have to do is to sit back and pray for God. Not because you're not powerful or you are weak, but it's because there is a thing called fate and you can't change it, no matter how hard you try.

Solearn when to save your energy, and learn the art of praying when it's not all in your hands.

I'm a Lebanese writer and I live in Lebanon. We were having a lot of political problems in our country, and we were trying to handle them and be powerful to overcome them.

Until that day, the 4th of August, when a massive bombing happened.

We heard it and saw the flames coming from everywhere. We went crazy and started to call everyone we know. We couldn't reach some people, so we started going down the streets, heading to the place where this happened without questioning why we are doing this.

I was working as a reporter for a tv station, and I headed down to cover the disastrous incident.

I remember pictures of people yelling, men and women, old people, children crying, roofs on the ground, and black faces with no hope all over the city.

There was a shock on everyone's face. I saw blood all over the ground and broken glass, and a teddy bear for a little child who must have died in this explosion. The face of that teddy bear was black and the eyes were crying, and I still remember it on the ground.

No one was understanding what was happening.

I didn't want it to happen. I did not want people to be killed and most of them to remain without their houses and shelters, but that was bigger than me and it happened.

Back then, I was having a relationship with a man with whom I felt something for four months. He was so kind and caring. I thought that was the man of my dreams in the way he talks, acts, and cares. He was a man of his word.

We did not choose to leave each other because I also knew how much he loved me, and how he tried to get me to be with him in the first place.

But this incident made us let go of each other.

Just those kinds of pictures, pressure, and feelings ended our passion somehow in one day. The explosion did not just let some people die or lose their homes; it made us all change from the inside. We are not the same at all after that day. Something died that day with the beautiful Beirut. A love that is much bigger than the love between men and women. A nation of love and mother land's love. We lost something and if I think about that day now, I think that what changed us was that we lost hope. We lost faith in our country and our leaders.

People wrote a thing that day and we all posted it "the people that died have survived and the surviving people have died"

We became dead from the inside. We had no more dreams, no future, we had no electricity after that, no petrol, no diesel, and no hospitals. We got nothing; we can't even afford to eat.

And you know what? After all that, I survived the year 2020.

I did it and those who have a powerful will and resilience did it also. I lost the best relationship I had in my life or maybe the best one till the moment. That is what I learned. I lost faith in my country. I see all my friends traveling and leaving this country. People dying and struggling, we are not working, and we all became poor. I was like a broken glass that looked at each broken piece and couldn't help myself to rebuild it. And we survived it all or some of us fought and built ourselves.

I survived.

I'm telling you this story because this is what you have to do.

Life is tough sometimes and you can't control the world and all the 8 billion peoplein it.

But you have the best privilege to control yourself. I used that.

I started rebuilding myself with priorities.

First, I ate well and slept well to be in good health. Then I went to a therapist to get it all out to relieve my mental health and then I added the things I love, need, and want like being around my best people and beloved ones, and doing some sports to get the stress out of my system. I also read some books to travel to another world, and best of all I imagined myself in a better place every day before I went to bed. So I visualized myself moving forward toward a better tomorrow.

And the most important thing I did was I started writing this book. So, *wanting a positive experience could be a negative experience; accepting a negative experience could be a positive thing. It all depends on the right timing. That is the best thing I could tell you, sometimes you can't make a move because right now it won't help, it's only a waste of energy. Sit and relax and things will fix themselves.* Sure, if it is a thing that you had nothing to do with or is bigger than you, why push so hard and lose your energy when in fact it's a bad day or a bad situation and it needs time? Learn to give time and be patient sometimes. Learn to be patient and wait for your turn. Somedays are just not yours and life isn't fair if every day is yours. Sometimes you have to be the one who is crying because someone has to laugh and be happy even if this person will be happy during your misery, he got to have some happy days.

We have to acceptthis nature of life or system and focus on what we have and what we could control and use it in the best way

If you watch the news every day, you will hear different sad stories. For example, if you hear about the man that raped that little girl and you couldn't work or eat all day, you have a good heart but it won't serve you and make you live. *Each and everyone has their problems, so don't make the whole world your problem because you will become the problem.*

Our lives are full of things that may distract us from what is truly important, we have to shut them out and have the power to be disciplined toward our targets and to achieve what we want to be.

We have to know first what are our priorities and what things we want to do and become, and those are the things that we should spend energy on and try to fix and give our attention to, or else it will be a loss of time.

Once I was reading a book, and the writer asked, "what are your values?" It really made me think about this topic and that when you have an answer to some questions, your perspective changes because you will know yourself better and know what you are doing. My values change from age to age and from one situation to another. I don't stick to things that may not help me now even if in old times I said I would never change things in me. Today it might be the time to change.

And I think it was a correct answer, at least for me. Sticking to some values or ways sometimes destroys you, you should know how to adapt and go with the flow. *Not every decision needs weeks to think about, some of our best decisions are the ones we take without even thinking about. In a blink.*

We have learned our values from our parents and neighbors, from school, from some of our teachers who influenced us, and from our best friends and their parents. We learned what should and should not be done, and the way our parents see things from their perspective. And I'll be talking about this more in the next chapters.

Then we grow up and face the world. Some of the "don'ts" should be done sometimes, and that's okay. It doesn't mean that you threw the whole system of learning that you got from your life, parents, and school. It means that you have learned a lot of things and now you are in a place where you should know what values suit you better than anyone who gave you their values. It's all about you, and it will never be about someone else.

You came here all alone by yourself, you took the first breath by yourself, and you'll take the last one all alone.

No one can stop that and no one is going to give you their breaths, days, or lives.

Life is full of knowledge, opportunities, and adventures. You'll take them alone, so fit them in the way you want. But never betray yourself and be someone that is not you, just because others want you to be that person. Stop wasting your time and energy there.

We are all actors in some place, and we do what doesn't feel like us sometimes, just to impress someone at a party for seconds, or to be a friend for someone, and even with the one we love, we try to be what they want at the beginning and that is what makes us fall apart in the end.

We are not what we show them. We are not that person that likes to go out and have adventures, but we saw that on their Instagram so we become the ones to do that with them, but in fact, we are the lazy ones that like to sit on the couch, drink wine, and watch Netflix all night without moving a leg. We could tell them who we truly are and still go to the places they want, letting them know that we are doing that for them. Out of our love for them, we should try to find a middle ground, not pretend to be someone else, and reach a point where we can't take it anymore and then show them the real us. Let us be real from the beginning and save ourselves all the trouble and pressure of pretending.

Be yourself no matter what. You are unique. You are what makes you "YOU" and there is no other you than you, so show your brand.

Your values are you no matter who is with or against you. You can change them whenever you feel you want.

Ask yourself what you want from life and then get a paper and pen and write what you did this week. Where did you spend your time and money?

There's the answer!

I don't care if you tell me family comes first, but you don't see your sisters for one month, that friends are not something important but you spend the whole week with them. You say you love your job but you are not working enough for it, not reading about it, or making any progress. *Your time shows where your loyalty lies.* Actions speak louder than words.

Success is nothing more than the desire of loving something with discipline to get better at it, then out of a sudden, the opportunity hits you, so you could be a master in it and succeed. But opportunity does not hit a place where it is not ready to be welcomed and embraced.

So, take care of what you want and where to spend your time, money, and energy. That is what you will become tomorrow.

You are the only one that is going to make you. You can get upset because your car's tire is flat or your t-shirt is torn. You can feel down because your friend is sad. You can make a big deal of a little problem that happened at work. You can make a big drama and be the drama queen of each day. But all of this is draining your energy and wasting your time, not mine or anyone's else. All these things are making you late for your big dreams.

Don't pressure yourself over little things and everything. If you want to be a victim of this life you can play this part all along the way. No one is going to help you, only you can throw this part and grab a new part to play in your life. So, stop making a big deal over everything and make everything hard for you. You can't fly and be free if you do this. Free yourself from what burdens you. Throw away all the little things and hold on to your target to get there as soon as possible.

Take a moment before reading the next chapter, and ask yourself what matters. When you have the answer, you will realize how much time you wasted on things that do not even matter to you deep inside. *Value your time, it's not coming back once you spend it. It's gone, as the breath that you just took now, it's gone. So, where and how do you want to spend it?*

Your time is limited in this life, live it the way you want. So, do you want to spend it in constant fear? That is what I'll be talking about in chapter five.

Fearing and trusting are similar in being extreme, be the observer

Part 1
Acknowledge and embrace your fears

Don't fear losing or failure;
fear living in constant fear

You are always competing with someone, always on the run. You are in a rush; many ideas are flooding your head. A lot of ideas are passing, you don't know how to stop them; you don't even know if they are real or not. Even in your most happy moment, you create something to worry about, and it's all in your head.

You hear me telling you more than once that it's all in your head, that gives you the power to know that you create what you put in there and what to throw out.

Try to stop these ideas and worries for a moment and think about why they are flowing. As I told you, *some things only need your awareness and insight so you can get rid of them.*

Some ideas and imaginations have no place, but you created them and put yourself in this situation and this constant fear.

Think of when and where you do not feel a little fear.

You're always in fear, in constant fear. Have you ever asked yourself why?

You will die someday anyway. If you fear or you don't, it is a fact and it will happen anyway. Fearing will not stop it. So why live in rush and anxiety?

You fear the new hello and last goodbye.

You fear the first day at school because you are the new one, and you don't know if they will or will not like you. You fear the teachers, whether they are nice or not, and the other students, if they are going to be your friends or not.

You fear the first week at work, what impression you are giving. You worry about if your boss is going to love your work or if your colleagues are going to treat you well.

You fear the first gym day because you are not familiar with the machines and how you can use them all, and someone that had been there for years may judge you. It's not your fault alone, it's our fault, all of us. We created this fear in others because we wait for a thing that we are good at and others are bad at, or are just still beginners in, to point fingers or show off what we are capable of. We want to show our areas of power because we know deep down that we have a lot of weak points, so we stand there to amaze others with what we can do in places where they can't do anything or are still new to discover how it can be done. But instead of giving them a welcoming hand and making them like the new thing, we scare them so they fear the new in everything.

When you become familiar with something, the fear will disappear. When you know that that guy or girl in the gym who is showing off, because you are new and they are experts, are doing that as a camouflage to hide their weak points in other areas, this will give you power over them and your first day at the gym will be a perfect day.

You always fear if your first date is going to be okay; if he or she will like you, if you'll look beautiful, if they will like your character, if they will see you as a good partner, and if they will be wanting to call you when the date ends without giving yourself the right to choose and decide if you will love them or like their attitude and actions.

Then you fear the last goodbye to the same person too, although at first, you feared meeting them.

You fear everything new, from not knowing where you are standing and where you are going. And you also fear losing some of the new things you were afraid to have in the first place. I fear it too.

Fear is hidden in our day-to-day life in small things and details, like being rejected or not liked by someone we like.

If there's one thing in the world that makes us one is that we all feel fear because we all want the same things. We want love, admiration, and respect. We want to be seen and liked. If we behave as we would like others to treat us, no one will ever feel this fear, but unfortunately, we don't.

Try to think about fear like a friend, understand its cause and the positive way of its existence. Be comfortable with the fear of new things and beginnings. Embrace your new experiences.

If there was no first day at school, you won't be educated now. If there was no firstday of work, you won't have a salary or experience now. If you didn't overcome the fear of that first date, you would not have experienced the best feeling in the world with that special person, and you would not fear losing this person beside you now. If the time comes for the relationship to end between you both, and you fear letting them go, you won't be able to welcome the next best person.

Life is all about changing things, jobs, education, and even people. You can't stand still in one place and watch everyone changing and catching opportunities while you do nothing.

There will always be a first time. No one likes it, trust me. We all love to stay in our comfort zone on our couches watching Netflix with our beloved ones. To overcome your fears, you must first know what they are. What are the things that terrify you the most? Feeling a little pressure because of new things is something normal that everyone experiences. Even the most confident people feel it, but they don't show it, so you feel that you are the only one who lacks confidence.

Remember what we said in chapter three? Fake it until you make it. Wear confidence as a mask so that no one can feel your insecurities. Then you could overcome hard situations positively.

Create a fear list. Think of the worst-case scenarios if things go wrong. Will you die? Think about what you can do to prevent the worst-case scenarios and do it anyway. It may go bad but you will not die, so you can try again, or you can prevent the worst from happening, or it might go right and you won't fear it again. But you can't know if you didn't try. That's why you have to take some risks sometimes.

When I lost my dad, I was upset because I didn't return the last kiss he gave me on my forehead, and I moved my face. I did not know that I will lose him and that he will be gone. After he passed away, I began acting differently.

I held onto people so tight because I feared losing them without saying goodbye or being nice to them. But holding on to people too tight makes my hands feel pain. It pained me more than letting them go. I acted for years in this way until the pain killed me, so I let them go. I realized that I can't live in fear; I can't hold longer onto things that have an expiry date. I can't control everything, and I should go with the flow. I don't and you should not always live in panic and fear. *We have to loosen our hands and what is ours will find its way to us.*

If we track our fears and their source, we will realize that our fears often are about things that we don't want to lose or things that we feel we can't live without, and losing them will make us suffer and feel lost. *But who said that losing sometimes isn't the same place where we find ourselves? Sometimes we have to lose our way to find the right way. Not everything we do is going to be as we wanted it. Sometimes life takes us in different directions, and then we recognize a new way of living and a new perspective of how we see things and how they affect us.*

We must learn how to master the art of detachment and then fear will not be our problem at all. We are related to attachment, and our need to control and possess things. *Remember that no one loses anyone because no one owns anyone from the beginning.* Parents don't possess their children even if they think they do, but they don't. *We own nothing. Everything is temporary in our lives, even the beautiful and bad moments are moments that remain as memories, and the second they pass they are gone and we can't relive them in the same way at all. They no longer exist. Clinging to temporary things gives them power over us, and they become sources of pain and fear. But when we understand the temporary nature of everything we are attached to in our lives, we can be aware of the moments we are living and be grateful for the opportunity that we are so lucky to borrow for a few seconds, hours, or days.*

Fortunately, fear is not always a bad thing, there's a good face to it. There is the useful fear that alerts us to move, do something different, change, and grow. Sometimes if we respond to it at the correct time, we can save ourselves from a lot of troubles.

Fear often helps us to identify and address patterns and behaviors that save us. It warns us of things, but we are misled by the signs sometimes.

We can use fear to get the best of us only if we can use it as a tool to obtain a greater meaning in our lives.

Fear of losing something shows us who we are at some level and what values we have and what things we want.

Acharya Prashant said in his book "Fear" that *confidence is fear and he means by this that sometimes when we fear losing something we become on the edge of our confidence.* For example, confidence is needed only when something important is at stake and we fear losing it such as an interview to get a job, so we try to act confident but we do not need this confidence to talk to a friend in a café.

When the football player has only one minute or he will lose the world cup, he gives the best of the best in him to score in the last seconds, and we have watched that happening

Even in marriage, we see couples having meaningless relationships because they took it for granted after years. They used to be around each other, but they no longer make effort for one another, and that is what made them fail and get divorced after a while, especially if neither felt or responded to the fear alert. Then when someone leaves the other, it makes the partner wake up out of a sudden and realize that he or she is losing something they took for granted for years because they thought they will always have it.

Even your mother in the house is the same case. You go out and follow up on a lot of things, work, friends, and relations. But you don't think of following up on your mother and what she wants most of the time because she's always there, and you do not feel the threat of losing her. Until she's sick, you feel that fear and start taking care of her. She's the most important and the closest to your heart, but you didn't think of her for once as a priority because you thought she will always be here anyway. But she might not be.

Some people don't take action unless fear threatens them to take action about things they must have taken action on a long time ago.

So sometimes it's ok to fear, it gives you a push if you know how to understand your fear and make it positive. Don't fear your fears, this is the biggest mistake and that is what will make you become a failure. Understand why you are feeling this fear, what is making you feel threatened, what will happen if you lose that thing that you are fearing to lose, what you can do to not lose it, and the faith you should have to believe that if it's gone it's for your good. You can gain better on your next try.

I can't tell you not to worry sometimes, because if I tell you that I'll be telling you to give power to your worries. Just stand there and observe the clouds passing, don't act on them, don't become obsessed with your worries, and don't give them the power and imagination to become real.

Just watch them and let them pass.

Don't fear your fears.

All you have to do to diminish your fear is to develop more trust in your ability to handle whatever comes your way. This is what I'll be talking about in the second part of this chapter.

Part two

*Have you ever given it your all,
and gone with the flow?*

Trust with love, and love with love, then trust and love will know the way back to you

I always had a problem with trusting others, I always felt that I have only myself to lean on. Maybe the life I lived made me this person. And I did not know what was happening because I wasn't talking to myself every day or feeling the damage inside me. I was distracting myself every moment I feel down or when someone disappointed me. I reacted to that by going out and partying, maybe sometimes by drinking and gathering with a lot of people without giving myself time to express the sadness inside me or the feeling of disappointment.

A lot of friends betrayed me and some of my relations too. Life in general betrayed me a lot in the past.

I lived a good life with my family. Love was the most beautiful thing that we had and we shared a very good bond. When I lost my father, I was fifteen, and I felt as if someone threw me into the desert at midnight.

My family was so loving, but at some point, everyone was busy with their lives. I went through a lot of lonely moments, and I did not have someone close by my side. Friends came in and out of my life, and for some of them, I did not belong to their level "money-wise". They had fancy cars, and they were the ones who could always go out, buy expensive stuff, and go on trips. It was hard for me to afford their lifestyle.

So, I lost a lot of them. I said it's okay. I'm proud of who I am and I'm trying to do my best with the things that I could do. But something inside me broke a little more every time I felt that I can't have the love and trust I want from those people that I love the most. The people that you loved unconditionally in your teenage years affected you a lot and losing them is hard. But when you are at that age, you don't notice what's going on inside you and that is what you see clearly after years.

It's very hard to have no one or not to trust that someone is going to hold you tight when you are falling. You feel like you are hanging on the cliff of a high mountain, risking that you might fall any moment.

Back then that feeling of never trusting anyone was hard on me. I always looked around me so deeply thinking about who will stay and who will leave. I always doubted the intentions of people around me.

Maybe that is normal from what I experienced with life and people. But it was so heavy carrying all this burden. It took away from me the best years and energy that I could have spent on something better. All that is because of the fear of losing someone, so I had to think about every word and action they did or said. And that was worse than losing them. Trust me. It was easier when they were gone.

I knew that I had only myself. But I didn't know what to do to help myself stop this fear and focus on what was important to me, until one night when I was watching an interview with the expert in relationships Mathew Hussy.He said, *"You don't trust that someone is not going to betray you, you just trust that you'll be able to handle it if they do." You should be able to walk away. Maybe you can't trust anyone. Time will only tell. That is a pointless waste of your energy and time."* I love what he said, and I felt it was true and it can help me.That night, I changed my way of thinking about things whenI believed that maybe I can't change people and make them stay or worry all the time if they will leave. *Worrying kills, it's the opposite of life and living. It's your biggest enemy.*

Today I don't blame any of my friends or ex-friends. I say thank you. You made me. And I don't blame my ex that betrayed me or didn't hold me so tight when I needed it the most. I say thank you. You people made me who I'm now, while you are buying fancy stuff and partying, I was studying life and every aspect of it to become the person I'm today. And while you are reading these words, my bank account is growing from selling my words of wisdom and making the world a better place with my approaches.

All it took me to do is to change my point of view towards things and to look at them from other perspectives. That was such a relief.

It was such a relief that I don't need to have someone. That "someone" should be me. No one should pay me all my bills or fulfill my dreams. I have to do these things by myself. I have to love myself and care about myself every day in every situation and make sure that I'm okay. And if not, I have to talk to myself nicely and encourage myself to be better as I do with beloved ones. When you can master all that, everything will be okay, and it's okay not to be okay sometimes. Time will take care of everything, *but only you can help you.* It's nice to have someone around whom you can trust and talk to. But it's only you who possesses the key to your happiness. You should only trust yourself fully, there's a huge magic in trusting yourself fully. This magic frees you from all worrying and fear because now you can face the wind no matter how hard it blows on your face. You know you will face it, you know the consequences, and you won't be so sensitive towards every betrayal because *you understand that people might pass as a season in your life and you'll benefit from their disappearing one day. And it all will make sense.*

We think when we are in a relationship that our partner will be there no matter what happens to us, but that is exactly the moment when we fail. Because no one is perfect, not even the love of your life that you chose and thought will do everything right. Everyone has his flaws, and there isn't only one person who can fill in for all your needs. That's why you have family, friends, hobbies, a career, and a love life. It's not all in your soulmate or your other half if you believe you are half. Everything good that comes your way is a plus. You have to be an independent person with a well-balanced life. *And what comes your way is a plus that might slip from your hands anytime. You have to live without it as you lived before it occurred and enjoy it as it lasts because everything in life is changing. What is yours now is mine tomorrow, so live it and enjoy it without worrying about losing it because you might lose it one day and the only thing you will regret about it is that you didn't enjoy it fully.*

Maybe you don't have to build trust with each and everyone who comes into your life. I think the magic is building trust with yourself. Trust yourself. Give love and trust to the world and do not wait for anything in return. Free yourself from the fear of losing. Spread your love and trust everywhere you go. You now know that you can trust yourself fully and if anything goes wrong, you will always handle it.

Say what you want, trust that God is there, then leave it for God. You are in good hands. If it is meant to be, it will be. Trust that the universe has your back and stop worrying. Trust with love, and love with love, then trust and love will know the way back to you.

The power of habits can influence whether we allow fear to control our lives or learn to trust in ourselves and our abilities. By consciously cultivating positive habits, we can develop the confidence and resilience to overcome our fears and trust in our own capacity for growth and success.

This is what I will be talking about in chapter six.

Chapter six

The Power of your Habits

You today, do you tomorrow

What are habits?

They are the small decisions and actions you make daily. They become a habit because you repeat them regularly and subconsciously. They might be things like brushing your teeth in the morning, taking a shower, or making coffee. They become a routine that you follow without thinking.

Habits can make you a very successful person and they can make your life so miserable as well if you pick the bad habits and get used to them. But whatever your habits are, the good news is that you can break your bad habits and adapt to the good ones instead.

According to researchers at Duke University, habits account for about 40 percent of our behaviors daily. This means that your habits take control over you. Moreover, they set a path for you to follow regarding your duties and responsibilities.

Also, think about this. Today you are the result of the habits that you have been used to for so long. So, pause for a moment and think about how happy and satisfied you are. If you are happy, this is good, but if you are not and you still don't feel that you should change anything, then this is a red flag. *Our habits become a part of our nature. They become engraved in us. We master them without thinking, which is why we should be careful about which habits we integrate into our lives.*

Habits contribute to shaping us and making us what we are. If you were playing basketball for ten years consistently, I think today you would be a very good player, if I don't want to say the best. If you did yoga for twelve years, you would be a yoga teacher by now, and you would be calm, eat healthily, and meditate. If you read books, you would have a lot of information that you can share. If you worked in sales for twenty years, you wouldn't leave the table without convincing me to buy whatever you are selling.

Some things we do become habits and we master them to the extent that we do them without any effort. For example, when you begin learning how to drive, you open your eyes so wildly, you keep your hands on the steering wheel, and you keep your legs steady where they should be. When you master driving, you will drive without stressing about these details because you will be doing it naturally. You don't focus that much while doing it. You mastered it.

However, the bad news is that you might have bad habits that you have mastered too and do naturally, like drinking alcohol, smoking, gambling, not eating healthy, sleeping very late, not sleeping enough, not exercising, sitting all day and night on your couch, becoming useless, and not working. Those are things you know you have to change but you don't know how because you feel that they control you. Try to start by removing the idea from your head that there is something in this world that can have the upper hand over you. Believe that you are the only master of yourself. Then, you have to learn how to transform your bad habits into good ones. When you learn to transform your habits, you can transform your life because the habits you have now will result in what you will become in the future. So, think of the image you want of yourself in five years and start now. Starting is not the hard part because it's easy to do, but the challenge is to be consistent and disciplined. Change takes time and effort, and it is the hardest part. Getting out of your comfort zone and what you are used to is hard. But no matter how much you struggle to change, you have to continue doing it.

Consistency is an essential component of success. So, when you stick to your plan and do not give up, you will transform your life and become what you dream of.

To break your bad habits, there is a procedure to follow:

1. *You have to replace them with good ones* because bad habits usually start from stress and boredom like wasting your time on some applications or drinking too much because you have nothing to do. But surely you know that you can do something beneficial and harmless when you are bored, such as studying something new, learning new skills, reading articles, and acquiring more knowledge about things you like to learn more about.

2. *You can rid yourself of minor bad habits by not being around places in which these bad habits occur.* For example, avoid going to the bar if you smoke when you drink. If you eat a lot of cookies when you are at home watching television, then don't buy cookies or don't watch television. If you text your ex, who has dumped you, when you are drunk, stop the hell drinking. If you lose your money when you play some games or gamble, don't go to the casino. If you already know the reasons that made you do these bad habits and I'm sure you do, why are you still doing them anyway?

I know it's not easy to change and adapt to change, *but if you are a dreamer and feel that your life is not going anywhere you want it to go, I think it's because you are not doing anything to change it. Change begins in your mind when you transform your mindset into a new one.*

It may be hard at the first but it will become easy. Picture the people you love to become like. Let us take Angelina Jolie as an example. For instance, you want to become her, you like her beauty and you love her body, but you don't take care of your body, and you don't exercise or eat healthy, but you still want a body like hers. After five years, you still want to be like her, but you are nothing like her because you did not change any of your bad habits to become even a little close to her.

3. Help yourself by picturing the life you want and surround yourself with people that lead the lifestyle that you want to pursue. Although this might make you feel bad about yourself and make you feel inferior to them, it will also motivate you towards reaching your goals. All you have to do is believe in yourself, don't give up, and never think that anyone is better than you. You can also have it.

Sometimes "but" is a useful word. Whenever you feel that you did something wrong, don't quit. Tell yourself, "I failed today, but I will try again tomorrow". So, stick to what you started with even if you failed several times. Soon consistency will become a habit, and you will be happy with how far you have come to achieve your goals.

4. Always be prepared that something might come up, and your plans might go wrong. However, always have a Plan B, so if you were not able to go to the gym early tomorrow, then go for a walk after work as compensation for the missed workout. Likewise, if you ate out today with your friends and had junk food, do not eat junk food the following week.

You can change your whole life by gaining a new good habit or getting rid of an old bad one. A habit can either make you a successful person or a loser. Big and great things are successfully achieved after you step out of your comfort zone and experience discomfort for a while, then these big and great things will be on their way to you. It is not easy to break a bad habit, but it is not impossible. It is all in your head as I said earlier. Keep that in mind whenever you feel like giving up.

5. Focus on your aim and be disciplined. I did that. I aimed to be a very famous writer, but I was addicted to playing cards for hours daily and all the time. That took a lot of my time. It was my comfort zone. But when I got back home, sometimes I used to log into Instagram and see a writer or a new book, and I felt so bad. I was very far away from my dream. I was not even doing anything to achieve it. Suddenly, I decided that I have to step

up and stop longing for my dream and start doing something about it. I had to start somewhere, so I started by writing quotes and paragraphs for months. Then I felt that I'm not getting anywhere and that this was not enough at all. I had to make writing a priority and be consistent. I promised myself that I'll be disciplined about this.

So, I got a pen and wrote on a sheet of paper that I'll write for one hour every day no matter how busy my schedule was. I started doing this and it became a habit. It was hard sometimes to find time or energy, but I did it anyway, and after several months I finished my first book. To do that, I found a place to relax to have the mood for writing. I used to sleep when it was time for everyone to wake up. I found that the early morning hours between four and six o'clock are the best times for me to feel inspired. I used to cancel brunch or be late for coffee with my friends because I woke up late. But I had to choose between waking up early and going out and having fun, or staying up late and achieving the dream of my life. I also created a mood for writing. I can't write in summer. I love to write in winter with the sound of raindrops; it makes me feel alive and inspired. So, I downloaded winter raindrop sounds from YouTube that I could listen to even during Summer. And that's what I'm doing now because it is still Summer and I have a timeline to follow. Now, that became a habit. I can't skip a day without writing or I would feel something is wrong. I need to write. I am alive while writing. I couldn't do it just for one hour, so I ended up writing for three or four more hours, and instead of finishing a book every three years, I'm finishing one every year now.

If you do nothing, nothing will happen. If you change a little, little will change. But if you take the right decision and stick to it despite the pain you will endure throughout the process, you will get there.

Everything you have right now is the result of what you did in the past. If your body looks perfect now, it's because you were always going to the gym and taking care of it. If you are graduating now, it is because you studied hard and tried your best. If you are a good mother, it is because you take good care of your children. Some incidents happen to us, that we are not responsible for, because of what we call fate. It's something bigger than us. But anyway, who we are now is what we did in the past. Here lies the importance of having good habits and integrating new ones into our system.

It's normal to feel that it is hard at the beginning because it is something new and we fear new things and need time to adapt. But don't think of the discomfort you are feeling now. Think about what this new habit will change about your life and how it will affect it positively.

In his book "The Power of Habit", Charles Duhigg says that habits are framed as an evolutionary way of saving effort. *If something is a habit, it saves brain power as we don't need to think about it.* He also sets the habit loop:

1. Cue – a signal to trigger the habit
2. Routine – a specific action or set of actions
3. Reward – the desired outcome

Bad habits are very difficult to eradicate. Instead, seek to change them, reprogram them, and rewrite them. The cue stays the same, the reward stays the same, and the craving stays the same, but the routine linking the cue to the reward changes.

You can't eliminate a bad habit, but you sure can replace it. So, choose a good habit as a substitute for your bad habit because to break a bad habit, you must start a new one. For example, if you want to quit smoking, try doing some breathing techniques, distract yourself by cooking, or go out for a jog. Engage yourself with something better and beneficial. Visualize yourself succeeding in destroying that bad habit, then smiling, and enjoying your success. Visualize yourself building a new identity.

My Man told me once that he used to take the same route to work every day, not thinking once of taking another. One day as he was on his way, the route was cut so he had to search for another. He found a new one because of this circumstance. He didn't choose that. At first, he was frustrated, but day after day he liked the new route, for he used to stare from his window and view new sceneries, and that was something he never really noticed or paid attention to before. After two weeks, the route he used to take was available again, but he didn't notice that until after two months.

Do you see? This is called habit. The most important part is that he did not think of changing something until he had to; something obliged him to change the route. The best part of it is that he preferred the new route. *Change is always an option and within our reach, so why not take the initiative to change instead of being obliged to change for some reason?*

However, beware of procrastination. Procrastination is the act of delaying our tasks until the last minute or even not doing them, thinking that we will always have the time to do them later. Procrastination is a bad habit that you need to beat right away.

We procrastinate on things that we find difficult, painful, boring, or stressful. It's often easier to avoid things that are hard for us to do. Joseph Ferrari, a professor of psychology at DePaul University in Chicago and author of "Still Procrastinating: The No Regrets Guide to Getting it Done" said: "Everyone procrastinates, but not everyone is a procrastinator." Contrary to popular belief, procrastinating has little to do with laziness. It's far more complicated than simply being a matter of time management. You can't manage time, what you can manage is yourself.

Ferrari doesn't believe in time management. As he pointed out: "There has and will always be 168 hours in a week. Not a minute more, not minutes less."

But I believe that you can manage your time only when you manage yourself, then everything will be managed and organized.

In 1956 the snooze button tool was first used and became many people's favorite. We tend to delay things thinking that we always have time. The first sign of procrastination is thinking: "I will start my day a few minutes later; I will just press this button."

We all want things to be done but always think we have time. Every day we postpone things till tomorrow and sometimes tomorrow never comes, or we wait for the right time and sometimes there's no right time. Then, we feel the heaviness of procrastinating, it often causes stress, guilt, and anxiety as a result of the loss of productivity or opportunity, which promotes even more procrastinating.

To beat procrastination, you have to understand what type of procrastinator you are. Is it coming out of fear of failure, or lack of willpower, or is it coming from not knowing your goals? There are a lot of things that may get in your way and make you procrastinate. Ask yourself about what is blocking your way, understand yourself, and you will be halfway there.

To reduce procrastination, no matter what type of procrastinator you are, you have to start by reducing the number of decisions you make throughout the day. Prepare yourself for some decisions the day before, instead of waking up and losing your energy on deciding what to do on the same day.

It is a waste of time when you wake up and start asking yourself whether you go to the gym, or meet your friends for brunch, and what outfit to wear for a meeting. Make those decisions ahead of time, and make this a habit to boost your productivity and prevent draining your energy.

So, plan your day in advance. It takes you a few minutes at the end of each day to write down what things you need to do the next day, or plan for the week ahead on a Sunday night.

Another method for avoiding procrastination is to set a goal or a target without setting an alternative if it's not done.

It's a tip by an influential crime-fiction novelist named Raymond Chandler. Chandler had difficulty sitting down at the keyboard and cranking out a predetermined word count every day like other successful writers, so he developed another method by sitting for 4 hours every day and giving himself an ultimatum: "write or do nothing at all".

This philosophy works for him, even if he doesn't feel like he can write. He made himself do nothing and get bored until he felt that he wanted to write.

I suggest breaking this down, to take a small action towards your target. For example, if you have a presentation, think about all the work involved. It Sucks right? Now think about a little thing that you can do that pushes this presentation a bit closer to being done. This little thing will motivate you to do more, and motivation will make you want to finish it and feel relieved.

Anytime you feel the procrastination creeping back again, you should take it as a trigger to chunk down whatever you feel like procrastinating on into something simple and doable.

Finally, the most important thing is to remove the cues that trigger your procrastination habit in the first place. If you don't work when there's noise, then don't work in public places. It is as simple as that.

To battle against procrastination, focus on your future, don't regret things you didn't accomplish. You don't want to live in regret.

"Once you know a bad habit exists, you are responsible to change it. NOW!"

Don't procrastinate, just do it now.

Our habits, including how we think and react to situations, can play a significant role in how jealousy manifests in our lives. By developing healthy habits and mindset shifts, we can break free from the cycle of jealousy and create a more positive and fulfilling life.

Breaking from jealousy will be the topic of our next chapter

Chapter seven

Jealousy is a mental cancer

The word "Jealousy" has no room in confident souls

In a world full of perfect images on social media, you might feel jealous, and you might envy some people. You wish you had the life that some people you admire have. You want a different you, you want to look like them, and you want to belong. You want a different nose and bigger boobs, and you wish you were taller to be a model and slimmer to wear things that don't fit you now. You want followers because someone has many of them, and can run any business and make it succeed because of the number of followers. We are living in a marketing world, with bloggers and influencers, where everything is possible.

You want a brand-new car as a gift on Valentine's from your fiancé just as someone's fiancé got her. You want the proposal she got and her best friend. You might also want to have someone's parents because of the picture-perfect you see on social media.

I understand, but you need to ignore all those images on your social media. They do not exist the same way that you see them. People post the perfect image of themselves. That couple might have been fighting for days, but they only show you the car gift. They might be broke for days, but you only see the dish, you crave, that they can afford once in a while. You want the body they have and envy them for it, thinking that God didn't give it to you because they are better than you. But you never know, you might have something you don't appreciate that they might kill for, or they might be struggling so much to have what you envy them for. So, you should either be satisfied with the blessings you have or work hard to get what you want if you want it too badly.

If you want it so bad, then get out of your comfort zone and do some effort. You will have the images they are posting, but you will bear the sacrifices they are making too. Then you will know that nothing is easy. *Perfect pictures are just not that perfect. They are just pictures. What's behind them is something that you don't see. You're just watching the perfect video after editing it and viewing the perfect pictures after photoshop.*

There are many types of jealousy starting from envying someone for things we don't have, to being possessive about things and people we have and don't want to lose, and fearing that our people might prefer others over us, that we think are better than us, and dump us for them. These insecurities both originate from the lack of confidence in ourselves and our low self-esteem of our worth and uniqueness.

The most common form of jealousy is jealousy about a partner we love. We fight for them, we fear losing them, we start being overprotective, we captivate our partner's freedom, and we ask and doubt them about everything and anything, just to make sure that they are not going anywhere. We think that by doing all that we would win their hearts and prove our love and loyalty, but that is not the way. It will make things worse. *Sometimes our insecurities turn out to be real if we think about them a lot and imagine them.* They make us look insecure and pitiful. No one wants to be around a needy person with negative thoughts all the time.

If you are jealous because you feel threatened when your boyfriend flirts with someone, and you feel you might lose them, stop being jealous. Put your ego aside. Your ego doesn't want to lose the battle. It won't let you feel safe or enough. It makes you feel that someone is taking your place because they have something that you lack, and it alarms you to do something because you are in danger and about to lose. You don't need to listen to it. *If you train yourself to love your uniqueness, you will never see anyone as a threat to you.* Even if you love someone so much, and they are flirting with someone else, you should not force them to stop it because if they know your worth, they won't do it in the first place. On the other hand, if they are being nice to someone and complimented them, it doesn't mean you are losing them.

You can be cool and confident and accept it. You might also find other people attractive and charming or love something about someone, and that does not mean cheating. You should not tolerate disrespect, but also you should not go into fights that lead to nowhere. Tell yourself that you are the bigger person and that you won't stoop to anyone's level. If your partner flirts with someone else and you sense disloyalty or cheating in the air, just let them be and leave.

However, always remember to take your time before acting on jealousy because it is tricky. Sometimes, it might all be in your head. Follow it back to its source. The problem might be in you, not in your partner. Whether your jealousy stems from insecurity, fear, or bad past relationship patterns, knowing more about it can help you figure out how to confront it.

Do the opposite of what your ego wants. Don't criticize the girl your boyfriend flirts with. He will find you more attractive when you do this. He will want to be around you more. He will be the one feeling threatened to lose someone like you with that bold character and confidence. Confidence is attractive and sexy.

Jealousy can destroy you, especially if you have very low self-esteem. To work on freeing yourself from jealousy, you have to read the first chapter of knowing who you are because when you know who you are, you know your worth. The chapter about confidence will also help you a lot to feel that *the only competitor you have to be better than is yourself in the past.* You don't need to look at others and what they have to feel envious. They have what they worked hard for and the good news is that you can also have what you want if you work hard for it, or if you work smart!

It is all connected, as every part in this book is connected to help you reach the ultimate happiness and satisfaction in life. To stop being jealous of others, you must first know yourself and your worth, and work on your confidence and self-esteem issues. You have to work on yourself step by step to release the bad thoughts and feelings that hold you back.

If you want to be a noble person, ask yourself about what your principles in life are. If your principles and values are to be understanding, confident, and powerful, then pick the higher ground. I don't think you want to make mistakes that show that you are small and pitiful, being jealous of other people. Jealousy is the opposite of being the bigger, more mature person. Jealousy is a very pitiful behavior. First, you have to acknowledge that it does not fit your standards. It's against your principles and values. When you view it in this way, you won't allow yourself to act in such a pitiful behavior.

Take a moment and think about what you look like when you are jealous of something or someone. How do you think you will be winning when you use the jealousy strategy? All you will seem as is a loser that can't stand their ground without someone and wants something that is not theirs.

When you are jealous of someone, jealousy makes you criticize them in a very bad way. You may convince people to see them the way you do. But what is the result of that?

You will become the smallest person in the world. You are comparing yourself to someone else just because you saw that they have something that you don't. So, you will humiliate yourself, degrade yourself, and seem petty, and that is what people around you will see.

I'm not saying that all kinds of criticizing are out of jealousy. Some of us might have fights with someone or a misunderstanding with some of our friends, and we talk about it with someone we trust to feel relieved, but that doesn't mean that we are jealous of every person we talk about.

Jealousy is a different thing. It's towards people that you think deep inside are better or luckier than you. It is when you want that girl's boyfriend, her clothes, her body, her mind, her money, her lifestyle, her business, or her success. When you feel deep down that you want what that person has, you start criticizing them for the things they have while you wish they were yours instead.

You try to make them look bad in front of your friends, family, or boyfriend. You don't want anyone to notice their beauty or achievements that you feel you lack. This is jealousy, but when you realize your uniqueness, this jealousy will have no room in your life. *Just like some people have things that you don't have, you also have things that they don't have or that they wish for. No matter what you think, God has divided blessings among all of us in a wise way. Trust that, trust him, and always trust in yourself. We all came in packages that differ in beauty, quality, way of thinking, kindness, and charm.* Don't let anyone ever make you feel that you are not worthy or less than others, especially the people who left you for others because that doesn't mean that others are better than you, it might mean that you are better than the person who left you or just different. *It doesn't have to be a competition, it is just life, and it is weird sometimes in a way that we don't understand, but one day we will.*

If you are a confident person and you know who you are and what you want, you will not allow yourself to become jealous because you already know your worth and that you are much more valuable than anything in the world. You don't need anyone's assertiveness. This feeling doesn't come from the outside, it's within you.

External things or materialistic things won't make you happy. If you want something you don't have and think that if you get it, you will be happy, you won't. Happiness comes from within.

The good news is that there's nothing that you can't fix. But you can only fix it if you face your problem. Start with labeling the things you are jealous about. Recognize them and analyze them objectively. When you become aware of your jealousy and understand its roots, then you will be able to end it. Because when you acknowledge your feelings, you can control them. You can remind yourself of loving yourself the way you are, and that you need no one to feel loved. That will stop you from feeling jealous of anyone you think is better than you because no one is.

When you change the way you think and see things from a different perspective, your envy and jealousy will vanish.

Trust me it is that simple. We tend to complicate things, but some things are simpler than we imagine. There are things that when you become aware of them, start disappearing immediately. All you have to do is to be aware. Always remember to practice gratitude for the things you have and the qualities that make you gain your confidence back. That will always lead you to peace.

For example, try to see that girl that looks like a model and has a wonderful body, nice clothes, and the most beautiful car as your sister. She's your sister that worked hard for these things. Don't you love your sister? How could you envy your sister and made her a bad person in front of people? Maybe your sister worked so hard and cried for nights on your shoulder to get these things. I'm sure if you look at her as a sister, you won't envy her, you will wish her the best of the best.

You should never be jealous of anyone's possessions because you don't know the price they had to pay in return. Think of a prostitute who sells her body to get all she wants easily. She might have everything that you don't, but don't you pity her for selling her body while your standards and values prevent you from doing the same? Would you be jealous of what she has? Of course not. She doesn't love herself the way you do, she doesn't know her worth when she did that. You have much more than what she got. Don't you see? However, in both cases look at her with love, and feel her pain beyond the perfect image. Imagine that she's you. You don't know what's inside her. If you were in her shoes, would you want people to envy and hate you because you have things they don't have?

Look at others with love, love is the best of God's creation. When you look at things deeply with a pure heart, you will not know hate or envy, you become clean from the inside and light from the outside. Jealousy will have no room in your mind or heart. You will conquer it. You'll end it.

Learning to let go of jealousy and comparing yourself to others is crucial in developing a strong sense of self and craving out a unique personal brand. By focusing on your own strengths and qualities, you can cultivate a distinctive image that sets you apart from others and attracts opportunities aligned with your values and goals. Your own brand is what I will be talking about in chapter eight.

Chapter eight
Be your own brand

***They might always tell you why
something won't work.***

Show them your way

All of a sudden you wake up one day and realize that the whole system that you built your life, values, and standard of success around is wrong. Totally wrong.

I'm going to save you time here, and tell you things that no one has told me before. I discovered them by myself through reading and a lot of research and experiences. I lived twenty-six years with misconceptions that dragged me down because I wasn't noticing what I was doing wrong until I really noticed that what was wrong was not the actions and decisions I was making, but rather the whole system we opened our eyes to. The things that our parents teach us to believe, and then we continue being lectured about throughout long years of schooling.

Obey and you will do good. Study hard and you will be the richest. Good grades equal graduating with high degrees and having the perfect job.

Thus, obey and you will be the best. Disobey and you will be the loser and be different. We fear being different. We fear being unique because we think it's wrong. It's good to follow what others are doing. It's safer to go with the flow and blend in. We might think that for sure if fifty people are sitting in a specific restaurant, it is because it is better than the empty one next to it. This might be true sometimes but not always. But we follow the trend because it is safer and we seek safety in life. No one likes risking their time, money, or reputation. So, we do what's already been done and tried.

But no, don't be a follower when you can lead and be followed. Don't be afraid to think out of the box and stand out. Have a mind of your own.

From the beginning of our school years, they start to teach us about the do's and don'ts. They categorize us as clever or dumb. Not only at school, but our parents also follow this at home. They pressurize us to study and excel in all subjects and lecture us about being quiet and obedient students. They permit us to talk and shut us up too. It is a whole system that instructs us to obey rules and treats us as slaves if we disobey any of these rules. When we are not clever or not good enough in some classes, they hire private teachers for us to help us master a subject that we struggle with or

don't like. They teach us to focus on our weaknesses and put effort to be better at what we are weak in, instead of becoming great in what we are already good at. They take away our energy and passion by forcing us to like and do what we don't like to do.

But why can't we be failures in many classes but great in only one? Why do we have to focus on our weaknesses and not work on our strengths?

Our whole system dictates us to follow and obey for years and years until we become in high school, and then they tell us to choose what suits us. We get confused about what suits us. They didn't allow us to have a choice before; they always chose for us. How could we suddenly choose and make decisions now? It's hard for us. It feels like we are thrown into the deep woods for the wolves. Most of us don't know what suits us because we got used to the idea that someone knows what's best for us more than we do. This is especially common in the Middle East where parents are still controlling over their children. So, when we go to get advice from our teachers or parents regarding which major to choose, most of the time they choose for us what is socially acceptable, and what suits them. Then we do it anyway, get the degree, and find a good job with a good salary as they told us to do. Then we discover after years that we feel like losers

because of the whole system starting from the first people we meet in this world, our parents, to the school system. They did not lead us towards this on purpose; they just did not know what they are doing to our future and they thought they were helping. In some cases, it really works, but not always.

The school system teaches us to become good employees and to do what we are told, but it doesn't teach us how to make money or become successful. It teaches us not to cheat on a test, cooperate, or commit mistakes, and that there is only one good answer for each question.

But how could we learn if we don't commit mistakes? How can we get the best of the best if we don't cooperate with others or brainstorm ideas or share visions? Why should we stay silent when we have a lot to say? Who said there's only one right answer for each question? There are a million answers.

I'm not saying that our parents and teachers want to destroy us, but they don't teach us to speak up for ourselves and do what we want. They teach us old ways that they think still work today. They don't get that we might fail in some subjects and succeed in others. In the end, we will succeed in one thing, the best thing that suits us and the only thing that we love and have passion for. They don't accept that we can't be perfect in everything. No one is perfect, and it's not our nature or mission to be perfect in everything. We are only human.

It might be too late sometimes when we realize that this system that we have been in for years is not the best as we were made to believe. After a long journey, we might have lost our energy and faith because we were programmed in this very wrong way.

I read a book not a long time ago. It changed the way I think about a lot of things.

Years ago, I thought that I can have only one profession in my life like being a lawyer. I thought it was wrong to have multiple jobs or have many businesses because no one taught me how to become rich and how it works until the man I love came into my life and recommended a book called "Rich Dad and Poor Dad".

I felt that this man came into my life for a reason, to make me the happiest in my life with his presence, lectures, sense of humor, and great mind. But no, not only this. He came to correct my beliefs in the whole system, to take me by my hand and make me face the truth, to stand by my side and show me what it is all about, and to correct my mistakes and give me back my power. This book taught me a lot of things, but the most important is having someone to talk it through with, discuss the ideas, and set a new plan. That was him.

The book was about how to have financial intelligence, and how to increase the assets I have and not the liabilities.

The book also taught me not to work for money, but to make money work for me. It taught me how to be brave and take risks, open a business, and try new things. We never know when it will be a hit for us.

We have to try several things. *Never say this is not going to work because there's always a way for it to work. We only have to discover the way.* We have to think and use our minds.

I'm not saying that we are not going to lose sometimes, sure we will, and this is one of the things we have to go through to learn and come back more experienced and powerful.

Life is made of opportunities, and there is always a good one around the corner. *There's always an opportunity passing through our days and moments. It's so close and all we have to do is to see it. Great opportunities are not seen with our eyes. They are seen in our minds. Great opportunities are ideas that pass through our minds that we don't even bother ourselves to think about deeply or use for our benefit.*

All we have to know is that there is no win without a loss. But to win, we have to be brave to try. Failure is part of the process of success. People who avoid failure also avoid success.I have never met someone rich who has never lost money. But rich people become rich because they master accepting a loss and turning it into a win.

We don't have to be perfect just at doing one thing. What they taught us was totally wrong. Today we can get the most expert team in any field we want. Because we can't be professional in everything, there are people for this.

I'm not saying that it is easy to change the ideas and values that we have been brought up with. We can change them only if we want to change. We can't teach an old dog a new trick. Unless a person is convinced to change, it's hard to change. When we believe that we are doing it wrong and that the old ways and techniques we used to do are not taking us anywhere, only then we will know that something is wrong and we will really want to change it. The world is filled with talented poor people. Because talent alone doesn't bring us money or make us rich, we need to know how to sell ourselves or our products and services. There is always a key for things and there's always a way in the little details.

The world is simply waiting for us to get rich. Only a person's doubts keep him poor. We must take our chances, and never let anyone make us doubt ourselves and our abilities. We should always try not to listen to poor or cowardly people. They will always tell us why something won't work.

The school system and the things we learned from an early age are so important because we become what we learn. So, we must be careful about what we learn and what our children will learn.

I advise parents to change their ways with their children and I ask school systems to give children the right to express what they love and what they want to become, and not to punish them if they did badly in some subjects or treat them as losers. If we are aware of all that, we could change a whole generation.

I also wish that we could add some courses for children in their early years in school, like how to build their confidence, how to attract good things, and how to be their own selves and think for themselves.

Our world needs a new generation with a peaceful and confident mind. It needs people who accept each other, clap for each other, empower each other, embrace each other, and make the world a better place. It is useless to fight about who is right and who is wrong. We should cease living in *competition with each other where we all want power and fame.*

Be yourself because this is the only thing that makes you special. We all are the same in many ways, but different in one way or another. That difference is our uniqueness. Let us speak our minds and make our own decisions. In this way, we will be ourselves, not a copy, not similar, not the same as anyone. It is us.

By cultivating a positive image and branding yourself effectively, you can attract positive opportunities into your life. When you project confidence, authenticity, and a clear sense of purpose, you become a magnet for positivity, drawing people and resources towards you that can help you achieve your goals and fulfill your potential. So, building your personal brand is not just about self-promotion, but also about creating a positive impact on yourself and those around you. That's what chapter nine is about.

Chapter nine

Switch to the happy mindset

Attract the future you want with a single positive thought: "You can"

I always defined life as opportunities even when I did not have one. So, God gave it to me.

Some may call it God's will and some call it luck. I call it faith; to have faith in God is to have faith in yourself. It's like something that you didn't see and you didn't touch, and you didn't even hear. But deep inside you know that it's hidden somewhere.

You pray for God to give you many things. But when you don't get any of these things, you start doubting if he ever really heard you or if he even exists.

I understand you. I've been there once.

One night I was feeling so down, and my whole world was broken around me. I felt like I had nothing to live for. I wasn't working and I was in debt. I was at the university and I couldn't pay for it. I was helpless and felt like I was a nobody. I felt as if I'm in a desert and wherever my eyes fell, there was emptiness. Not knowing where to begin and not feeling that it was even possible to rebuild, life back then didn't seem to me like a nice thing, and I enjoyed nothing in it. I started questioning myself if anyone was hearing me or sensing the hurt I have inside. I even questioned God and asked him, "Why is all that happening to me? Are you there? If you are there, why are there people dying of hunger? Why did you create them if this is their fate? So how could you hear or help me? It seems you won't."

I felt that I wanted to end it all here. I wanted to end my life so all those feelings will disappear so that I could live in peace somewhere else in a better place where the sun touches my body and enlightens me with love and excitement.

I stood by the window and looked up at the sky. "Allah w Akbar" echoed from the mosque. I felt as if God is telling me that he is capable of saving me and he is there. As if that was a sign telling me to hold on a little bit more. It was something larger than life that made me feel that I should hold on and that better times are coming. It seeped through every cell in my body, heart, and brain. I did not know what was this feeling and how I got the power suddenly to feel that everything will be okay, while I felt that I had lost everything moments ago. I had no job, I couldn't pursue my dream of studying, my last relationship was a disaster, and I was not close to anyone. I was all alone and suddenly a leap of faith just made me stronger.

I think it was "faith". I'm sure it was. It is the faith that God sent me. Faith in him, and faith in me. If we don't believe that God is there somewhere hearing us and our prayers, how could we survive?

Not everything is mathematical, some things are mysterious, and their beauty lies in their mystery. To feel and have faith that there's an upper hand who's seeing everything and feeling everything is comfortable. People who don't believe in God consider the people who believe in him, cowards. They think that those people are not brave enough to face life all alone by themselves, so they always depend on God. I'm not here to convince you that there's a God, you are free to believe that there is not. But I can tell you that I've felt him in my heart. He gave me love and comfort. I believe in him and have faith that he's always there for me, not because I'm afraid to be on my own but because I love knowing that he's always here when no one will be.

I believed in him more and more because of the power that hit me all of a sudden, the moment I decided to end my life. A strange and strong feeling made me change the way I was thinking in a blink, and I called it the moment of faith.

After one month after that night, my life changed in a very nice way. I found a job and continued my studies. Things were fixed by themselves. It turned out to be a nice life full of excitement and things I love. After feeling that it was the end, *I believed that sometimes we can start from the end.*

That's not the important thing. The important thing is that I felt it inside. I felt the faith in God, I felt the faith in me, I felt *that there's something always on its way, but it cannot reveal itself if it is not the right time.* You have to be ready and aware of every sign around you. You have to feel it, and *when you believe in it, you attract it.*

I felt that when I believed in God and succumbed to him, I believed in myself. Then things started to change in a short period after being stagnant for one year. Things started to fall into place and everything seemed nice to me again in a much better way. I felt that I'm attracting everything I want. I'm shining wherever I go. I'm happy, and confident, and there's abundance in everything I wanted everywhere I go.

And this is the law of attraction. I am sure you heard about it a lot before. But some of you did not believe that it was true, or maybe it did not work for them, so they did not believe in it.

But to make it real, rule number one is that you got to have faith in it. You have to trust it fully and send what you want to the universe and believe that the universe will give you signs and opportunities for what you asked for if you open your eyes widely and listen carefully.

Do you ever ask yourself why people who believe in "reincarnation" experienced it while it does not happen to those who don't believe in it? Think about it. One day you'll have your answer. You don't need my answer here because it is about what you believe in and not anyone else's beliefs.

When you believe in something without doubting it at all, it starts happening to you. And when you think positively, you attract more and more good thoughts and you start imagining the things you dreamed about and believe are true. You visualize them as if they are real and that is when you will start to be ready to welcome what is good for you and what is set out there for you in the universe. For example, if you want to be a doctor and you don't see yourself doing it one day in your imagination, you won't do it for sure. *To achieve, you should conceive.* Start trying it with little things. Ask about what you want, and be specific about what you want. Feel it, believe that it relates to you, you own it, and you can be it. Imagine yourself having it. And the most important thing is don't give up if you didn't receive what you want on the first try. You have to master it like any other thing in life. Mastering the law of attraction needs time and faith.

On my trip to Antalya, I was so excited and I wanted to leave the airport and meet my beloved ones outside. So, I was in a rush and waiting for the bags to show up. I said out loud to the universe that I want my bag to be the first bag. Time passed and all people were waiting. I visualized that my bag will be the first bag and I imagined myself carrying it and walking away. The bags started showing up, and my bag was the first one in line. It worked, it worked! I focused on what I wanted, asked for it, and visualized that I got it, so I deserve to get it and I got it.

The rhythm between you and the universe is so special when you get along. You feel it is working for you. It opens good doors and closes bad ones. It gives you abundance everywhere. You are dancing and singing in the clouds.

That's why I believe in visualizing, it has a big probability to happen and even if it doesn't, it gives you that sense of positivity and a good mood to accept whatever happened and accept it as a win. It's a healthy thing.

Close your eyes every day in the morning before getting out of bed and visualize for 15 minutes. Imagine your day going as you planned, and that what you plan every day will make you reach little by little what you want to be in the future. That will make you focus on good things in your life, and it will make you imagine the events that you want to happen throughout the day. That is what will attract them. People always make a mistake by imagining things that they fear, and the more you give it a thought, the more power you grant to it to attract it to your life. So, stop attracting bad incidents because you imagined them in the past.

Stop worrying because worrying is not more than an unhealthy mental habit, you do not need to be a victim of worry. Empty your mind from your worrying and fears and replace those thoughts with positive ones. If you feel this is hard, ask God for help because he's always there listening. He can do whatever you ask for if you believe in him and his power.

Attract what you want and whenever you feel a bad thought is coming your way, block it in any way or replace it with a good one. Don't give it power over you. *You create your life with your thoughts. So, mold your thoughts to be in your best interest.*

We are a lot more worried about losing what we have, rather than getting what we want. That's why most of us subconsciously play not to lose, instead of playing to win. That's why we don't win and things we want don't happen. Because we focus on what we are afraid of and not what we want, we give the negative thought power over the positive one.

If you are starting a new business, you fear failure so you start thinking about how not to fail. So you start focusing on what you don't want to happen and give it the power to happen because you are focusing on it.

Thus, try not to focus on what you don't want and do not like. Stop limiting yourself to "what if" worst-case scenarios. You don't need to do that. Why don't you use "what if" for the positive scenarios?

To conclude, think positive thoughts, prepare for success, pay attention, be aware of opportunities, and you'll be there.

"Similar" attract?

People say that opposites attract. That can be true. But it's more often that "similar" attract. For example, you are more likely to attract people who are wealthy and have fancy cars if you are wealthy and you have a fancy car. Also, you are more likely to be in a group of beautiful girls and models if you are beautiful and tall and you are taking care of your outfits and looks. You can't be a businessman or businesswoman if you are around a bunch of losers, but you can't be a loser and not think about making business if you are around great minds and people who are successful in their business. So you attract what is similar to you without knowing that.

However, what it means is that our thoughts attract what we achieve. This is simply because we tend to do what we think about and believe. Our actions then produce the results we have in life.

Limited and negative thinking leads to limited action. If you think that you are poor and have no money to buy brands and be like one of those bloggers you like and follow on Instagram, how would you gain that money? If you don't believe that you deserve it and that it's coming your way, how could it come?

You should start to eliminate the negative thoughts you have and replace them with positive thoughts and beliefs. Then work on making the positive beliefs feel like they are true.

But don't get that wrong. The universe doesn't want you to be needy and nag all the time about what you want. Just ask for it, relax, and imagine it.

They say that "If you don't need it, you are more likely to attract it." If you are a needy person, no one would like to be around you. A lack of something attracts more lack and vice versa. This is why *debt attracts debt, and money attracts money.* That's why you should always clear your path and your way for the life you dream of. You should dispose of things that hold you down like your thoughts that you are giving the power to destroy you. So, to lead a healthy life, you should always create a space for new things. *To do that, you must first get rid of your negative thoughts. You have to have a new mindset and to have a place for fresh and positive thoughts because positive thoughts and energy don't stay long where they don't belong, and they will never belong to a mind full of negativity.*

You always see beauty in others and never observe your beauty. For example, you are watching tv and you see some celebrity on the red carpet or some big businessman and you think about how confident they are. You think it is for sure because they have money, or because they are famous, or both. No actually. Maybe neither is the reason for their confident character. The secret of successful people is that they believe in themselves, and their worth. They know that they are unique and they believe that they came to this life to offer something of value to the world. They are not any better than you. You can do that. And you can be there.

But you are not a believer. You are a dreamer. Dreams without the vision of a believer remain dreams only.

Life gives you opportunities but it is not like you trip over them while walking on the street. You endure a lot to have them. You have to believe in yourself. The more you believe that you can, the more you are close to getting what you want.

In every second of our existence, we act as human magnets sending out our thoughts, vibes, and emotions and attracting back more of what we have put out there. So be careful about what you put out there. But very few people are fully aware of how much of an impact the law of attraction has on their life.

How did I first believe in the law of attraction or hear about it?

Hundreds of years ago, the law of attraction was believed to be taught first by the immortal Buddha. He wanted *"what you have become is what you have thought"* to be known to the world.

I did not find out about the law of attraction through Buddha though, but I was first exposed to it through a book. When I was seventeen, I worked with a Lebanese director as a secretary. His name was Said El Marouk. I knew nothing about his private life and I did not bother to ask. One day he came to the office and saw that I was not working or doing anything, so he told me to come to his office. He asked me a few questions about my life, and he seem interested. Then I asked him about how he became a famous and well-known director. He told me that his mum and dad are deaf, and it was not easy growing up with deaf parents. But he did it anyway. I further asked him how he was able to make it, and he pointed to a book and asked me to read it. That was the turning point for me.

So, I took the book and went to my office, and in 8 hours during my empty schedule that day at work, I finished that book. The book was titled, "The Secret" by Rhonda Byrne. She talked about the law of attraction in her book, and how it can affect life and change it.

To utilize the law of attraction, you must think about the things you want to become and want to be, not the thing that you fear and want to avoid.

I loved that book, and it had a special place in my heart because it was the first book I read that affected and inspired me, andthe first one in my journey of reading psychology books and writing about it.

Byrne wrote about three steps in the law of attraction.

First, you should ask for what you want and put it out there in the universe. Then all you have to do is believe in yourself and in being able to do it. Visualize yourself doing it and then you will receive it.

Ask and be specific about what you want. If you want a million dollars, write on paper that you are grateful for having a million dollars and act as if you do. If you want to be an actor, write that and visualize yourself as an actor walking on the red carpet. *If you don't have unwavering faith in your goals, how could others believe in you?*

So, I wrote down that I want to be a famous writer, a writer whom people will remember for her quotes, and speak her mind. I kept this paper, and I still have it today.

But even though I read it all, I did not work on it or believe that much about it back then. So, I am not surprised if there are still people who don't believe in the law of attraction and don't try to make it a part of their lives. As for me, I was lucky that the incident I told you about earlier when I felt that faith suddenly. From that moment on, something changed inside me and I had that faith in attracting what I want.

Second, the law of attraction asserts that whatever you focus on will grow. Visualization is one of the most essential tools. You must make your visualization as realistic as possible.

Think positive, visualize things that make you happy, and enjoy being happy. Even when things go wrong, train yourself to see the positive in everything.

Your thoughts are a type of nonphysical energy that affects your physical world. If you want to be happy, you have to tune your thoughts and feelings toward happiness. The easiest way is to create positive emotions of joy, appreciation, and gratitude. Practice these emotions to get what you want.

Third, what you think about and give thanks for, is what you will bring about.

When you worry, worrying simply creates a negative expectation. When you worry, you're creating images in your mind of what you don't want. You don't want something, but you are expecting it to happen and thus worrying about it and attracting negativity.

The law of attraction states that you will attract whatever you give energy to whether u want it or not. Therefore, you must consciously control what you think and feel.

You can use your thoughts and energy to produce positive outcomes. But the problem is that we are unconscious most of the time, and we are thinking about many things, maybe negatively. So, we give things that we do not want to happen power over us.

On the other hand, when we are aware of our feelings all the time, we are focused. That helps us realize the bad and negative thoughts to stop them and replace them with good ones. Imagine it, feel it, and be grateful for it before it even happens to you. Only then you'll deserve it. You will be happy, and people will recognize your light and will want to be around you. You will start attracting people and opportunities because of your openness and your light. All of this can happen because of positive thinking and healthy thoughts.

So, whenever you find yourself worrying, replace this negative thought in your mind with things you love that make you happy.

I always thought that men are bad and that one day they will do me wrong and break my heart. So, they did until I met that man who trusted me without doubting me, and didn't question me about anything. He talked about marriage and children from our first month together. I asked him about how he could trust that we would end up together. He told me that he would rather think positively, that we want each other, and that he believes that we will marry soon. Even if God's will was not to make that happen, at least he would have a good trustworthy relationship with me as it lasts, and that negative thinking is a waste of energy, That made me more responsible towards him and our relationship and made me believe I can make it work out and think the way he does. I started to think that tomorrow we will get married and we will live happily ever after if that is what I want. Even if our relationships don't end up in marriage, what is the use of thinking negatively about a partner, thinking of being cheated on or betrayed? Why do we create a bad scenario and anticipate it if we don't want that to happen? By thinking of the bad ending, we attract it. It didn't happen alone; we called it and waited for it. So try from now on to wait for and attract the good things and the happy endings that you dream about.

Some people come into your life and teach you something that will turn out to be an opportunity and a fortune if you listen carefully. That man was my fortune and he still is. Don't miss your opportunity. *God blessed you with two ears to listen better and one mouth that you should use to utter words that people will remember and appreciate. Make your words significant so someone will thank you even without you knowing it, as I thank this man for life.*

Think positive and you will be happy and positive. Make your world spiritual and positive so that positivity will always find its way back to you.

A positive mindset can greatly enhance your ability to master your talent. By approaching your practice with optimism and can-do attitude, you can unlock your full potential and achieve success.

Mastering your talent will be discussed in the next chapter

Chapter ten

Master Your Talent

***It might be possible to fly without wings,
but it's impossible to soar so high without
knowledge and skill***

Talent consists of the abilities that we are born with, it's something built in that you love and that you master with practice. Without practice, it remains talent and won't disappear, but it won't grow.

If you still can't identify what's your talent, ask people around you what they think you do the best, or try to remember what compliments you usually receive and what they are related to.

But I'm pretty sure if you apply this book from the beginning and ask yourself every question in chapter one, you will have an idea by now about what your thing is.

Mastering a thing should not be considered something insignificant, it's the biggest challenge you would ever do in your life. When you put time and effort into something, you give it your soul, time, and life. Time is irreversible.

Mastery means to have great skill at something. For example, if you are fluent in French, you have mastery of this language. If you win every chess game, you show mastery in the game. So, the feeling of mastering something is big, and it makes you so high while doing what you are best at. It's very positive to have this from time to time, it boosts your energy and makes you more confident because you are playing in your field. But to feel this high, you must first give it your time and energy to be a master at it.

So be careful in what you choose, choose from the heart and only the heart what will make you happy. Knowing that mastering your talent needs you to be open-minded first and master the art of learning.

You have to welcome new techniques and approaches, learn, take criticism, work hard, always try, and challenge yourself always to be where you want to be.

Malcolm Gladwell, the writer of outliers, says it takes 10,000 hours to achieve mastery. That means if you want to master anything in life, you have to give it hours and hours of practice.

If you are willing to do that, you will master it. But no matter how much time you put in, and even if you master your thing, mastering will always be temporary, and that's the magic. You always feel that you need more doses of what you master because things are changing so quickly, and in different directions, so you have to be fast and flexible. You can't master playing tennis when you are ten years old and assume that you will still master it when you are thirty when you stopped practicing it for twenty whole years. You have to always give it the time and energy to always be a master in it. If you love a thing, you should work hard to master it and never stop any day because you will always have more to work on mastering in a new way.

So, when it comes to mastering a thing, the first question you should ask yourself is, "would I be willing to commit a lot of time to this activity and live with it all my life?"

I'm not saying that you should come to this life for one thing only, on the contrary, I already explained to you about your eight areas of intelligence to let you know from the beginning that you are more talented than you imagine. You can work on all of your talents, but what I'm saying is that you should master one thing before working on another. Do not go in many directions at once because you won't arrive at any of them.

If you try to catch two mice at the same time, you won't catch any, or the possibility of catching any of them is less than the opportunity if you focus on each one at the time.

It's not impossible to be a doctor and an actor at the same time, and you might own a restaurant and be a businessman too. Also, you can be healthy and go to the gym and have a perfect body. But it is impossible to be an actor and a doctor, a pilot and a lawyer, and a model all at the same time and succeed in them all. You are human, you have feelings, time to sleep, a family to love, a life to live, and things you do that inspire you spiritually. Everything needs its time. You cannot take your light and others' light. That's why everyone has their unique power and talent. You can't take everything from everyone. This is so selfish and greedy and cannot happen. You can always hire the best of the best in each of these professions, they don't need to be done by you. But you cannot have the talents of each person in this world. It's not your dream to fulfill, it's theirs. You can always try new things, even if you suck at them, trying new stuff. Having adventures is a very healthy thing too. It makes you feel always alive, and it helps you to know what you love most in your life. You can know the value of the thing you do when you try another and feel that it is not your thing, even if it is fun.

You can be anything and you can be many things if you understand how to master it. Don't work on being a writer, a yoga teacher, and a doctor together because each needs its time. You can study to be a doctor for years and write at the same time and do yoga as a hobby. But it's hard to be a yoga teacher, go to a yoga class every day for five hours, attend university classes to be a doctor for 7 hours, and write for 3 hours a day. *Multitasking will damage you and ruin your passion.* I'm not saying it's impossible. *I'm saying take it slowly, live the journey, don't rush, and don't go in many different directions.* Master one thing in every stage of your life. One day you will be good in all things you like and want if you are that multi-talented person and you have that gift.

So, the key is to master every single thing at a time. Focus first on being a doctor, write for one hour a day as a hobby, and take some yoga classes in your free time, then when you graduate and become a doctor, take more yoga classes to become a yoga teacher. After you feel that you mastered yoga and you can teach it and it became an easy thing, start writing every day for long hours. Maybe after 5 or 6 years, you'll become a master in these three professions.

That is what I want you to do even with small things. Don't go to the gym, send an email to the client that you forgot to send earlier, make plans for tonight's outing with your friends, and search for a new restaurant on Instagram all at the same time. The email might go wrong, your choice of restaurant for tonight might be bad, and you won't have enough time to take care of your physical appearance before the outing which will cause you more stress. Do one thing at the moment. *Live in the moment with that one thing you are doing. Give it the right to be there, to feel it, to do it right, and master it. When you rush something, you don't enjoy it, and when you don't enjoy the process, you won't get a good feeling out of the result. Try to be aware of whatever you're doing. Every moment matters, it's not going to come back. Never.*

I'm a writer and I have been writing this book for one and a half years. At the same time, I go to the gym and do yoga. Those are my hobbies. I love doing these things, they inspire me. I read a lot of books and got inspired by each book. I love words and the meanings of each word, and I believe that every word has a different perspective for each person who is reading it because it reflects what we take from it and what our souls require. *A single word could change a whole person if it touches him deeply and if it was the thing that he was searching for in order to change.* That is how much I believe in writing and words. So, I wasn't ready to do anything while writing each book or play because I used to think I can't. I wanted to focus on each word and how I deliver it. I wanted to stay in focus, I couldn't think of anything else, it will ruin my spirit and imagination.

But out of a sudden, I got inspired by someone close to me. He convinced me to do one thing aside that suits me, I was interested in doing my brand of tanning oil and skincare collection because I used to take very good care of my body and skin. I adored my body and every detail of it. I used to pamper myself always, and besides, I have tanned skin. So, I did my research well, and I asked experts about it. I gathered a lot of information from a lot of sources until I felt that I'm ready. Even in the feeling of readiness, there was some risk. Some people told me not to do that because everyone will get confused about whether I am a writer or a businesswoman. I call those people the "don't" people because they always see that whatever your idea is, it's not going to work. Don't listen to them and prove yourself. Love the process and master it, and you will be ready to do some business and spice up your life. It's healthy to grow and not be stuck in the same field your whole life. Thus, it became a plus in my life, and it added to me a lot. After I was fearing change or giving my attention to anything else other than writing, I discovered that I could do it easily. Just when you master one thing, you can start adding new things to master.

So, before I publish this book and while adding the final touches, my tanning oil and skincare brand "Seraz" is already out there, and I'm so happy with the result. It's traveling from one place to another. It's working so well and I love that. It also inspired me a lot in writing. After thinking that I have to add the final touches, I added much more to this book because I felt that I'm powerful inside and capable of handling a lot of things artistically. That's what is called mastering a thing.

Success inspires you more and makes you more productive in every aspect of your life.

Start by writing every day what the most thing you think about is, what you imagine you are doing in the future, and what the life you want looks like. But that won't work if you want the results without the process and if you want to be successful at things that you don't enjoy doing. Then this will be the wrong call.

The true call is the thing that you enjoy doing. You feel that this is where you belong. Even while doing the thing that you are passionate about; you sometimes feel tired. But that is okay because nothing is easy to get, and the real passion inside you won't let you stop even if you are tired because that is your thing. Stick to it when you find it. You can't find it if you didn't try and give it a shot.

Life is about opportunities and I believe in luck, but you can't wait for luck to save you. You have to start from this moment even if you have nothing in your hands. Start with nothing but at least start. Success won't come knocking on your door, offering itself to you. Success is a passion for something that needs practicing, acquiring knowledge about it, and gaining experience, then boom the opportunity will meet you on the way when you are ready to receive it and act on it.

We always hear the phrase "work on your weaknesses to become better". This is a wrong idea. Never give power to what you lack, give power to what you are good at. Know your weaknesses and try to be okay with them, no need to work hard and be perfect to impress anyone. It is okay to try even if you don't see yourself in some fields, but it is not necessary to be good at everything. Work hard on your strengths because someone else has your weaknesses as strengths built in them, and they are succeeding because they are their passion. *They are born with the talent that you lack, and you are born with the talent they lack.* So work on your passion to succeed in it. I don't need to be a chef to have a restaurant I can be a businesswoman and invest in a restaurant and a good chef. Cooking is the chef's passion, not mine. So why should I steal it and pretend to have it or work hard for it? It's just not in me.

Accept that you don't have to be good at everything. Just be the best in what you like and want and be happy about it, and let everyone be what they want.

That is what successful people do and that is why a successful person applauds another successful person from the heart. People who take a shot in their field consider that their only competitors are the other people in their field, as well as their own selves, being better tomorrow than today.

So, the chef is not my competitor as a writer. He needs to read some of my quotes and advice, and I need to taste his delicious food, feel every detail in his dish, and enjoy it.

Invest in your strengths, and you'll achieve depth, meaning, and satisfaction in your life. Work hard until one day you'll be so good that no one can ignore you. You are there. You exist powerfully. Your skills, talents, and reputation talk about you without you even talking.

While mastering your talent can bring a great sense of fulfillment and purpose, it's important to maintain balance in your life to prevent burnout and maintain your well-being. By finding ways to incorporate hobbies, socializing, and relaxation into your routine, you can recharge your batteries and stay motivated to continue honing your skills and pursuing your passions.

The art of balance will be the topic of the next chapter

Chapter eleven

The art of balance

To have a little bit of everything you need is all you need

You can master all those arts and be a good master in them only if you master this: BALANCE

I think this word would be my next tattoo.

We all talk about balance; we hear it everywhere but we don't know how much this word is powerful and how it affects our lives. We just say balance is very important but we don't balance. It's very hard to balance, it's not an easy thing but it is an art. Even art lovers don't master this art. Because when they are doing art, they forget the whole world sometimes for days, months, or even more. That's why it's hard to balance when we love what we're doing, or when we are going through a phase of addiction to something, we can't balance, we just want what we love and what makes us happy now. I agree, I always advise people to die doing what they love. But to live a proper and happy life, we need balance to grow and truly live even if we don't notice it sometimes.

To have a little bit of everything you need is all you need.

Living a balanced life means determining what is most important to you and expending your time and energy accordingly.

Organize things you feel that you want at the perfect time. Don't overwhelm yourself or do anything during the time allotted for other things.

You need your time alone as much as you need your social life activities. You need to sleep as much as you want to stay awake and live your life. You need a diet as much as you feel hungry and need to eat. You need balance no matter how much you feel that you can't get enough of a specific thing.

A balanced lifestyle reflects that the different elements of our life are in the right amount and proportion. Adopting a balanced lifestyle is very important because it has immediate and long-term effects on our health and well-being.

The importance of a balanced lifestyle is something most people take for granted. Living a balanced life is very healthy for one's personal and professional growth. Many people think that it's hard to balance a lot of things like a love relationship, taking care of a new career, and attending all family rituals, but the truth is that it can be a lot easier to do than most people think, and it much better for a healthy and happy life. I know when we are new in a relationship, we just want to be close to the person we have feelings for, it's where our heart is happy. We want nothing more than this, but that is what leads us to a boring relationship after a while because becoming too connected to someone in a short period, makes us or make them feel after a while that our life or theirs has changed suddenly. Although it may look nice at the beginning, we will feel that we want our life back after some time. Here some of us feel that our partners changed, and we start to panic. True, they might have or we might have changed because we rush into things and some of us don't know how to take it slowly after that. As a result, we might break up with our partners or they might breakup with us. Then we start to question ourselves why. Why are all our relations ending in this way? Well, it's our own doing. We don't know the art of balance, and we don't adopt it in our lives and every aspect of it.

Let me say that you attended a party, and you loved it a lot. You are drinking, dancing, chatting, and enjoying yourself still while everyone is leaving. The people who invited you will get bored of you, they want to go to sleep, but you are still there. You won't be on their next invitation list for sure. You didn't read the vibes.

You did not balance between having fun and knowing when your fun night should end. You did not know when to leave. *You have to know when to end the party.*

Usually, at the beginning of new things, we always overdo them and ruin them. For example, you have a family ritual, but you want to spend your day with your new man, you feel excited to meet him but guilty to cancel on your family. Fearing that he might find another person who will give him more attention, you decide to be with him and miss the family ritual.

You don't have to upset your family or lose your new good and romantic boyfriend. *If you balance and organize, you won't have to lose something because of something else.* With balance, you can get the best of everything and be a happy person with a beautiful peaceful life.

So attend your family rituals because they show respect for you and your family, and then make it up to your boyfriend. He will understand, respect you more, and will still be around after months. He won't vanish into thin air if you act in your life in a balanced way because you are only attractive when you have balance, and no one will get bored of you.

When you balance, you show strength in your character. Having a strong sense of controlling one's life is a predictor of positive feelings of well-being more than any other factors of life we have considered.

Being organized is very important to help you keep a clear mind and help reduce stress. It gives you space to plan things, as well as time for all the tasks you have, and makes room for the things that you enjoy in life.

You will be a happier person when you can manage your time and organize your life. You don't have to give up on something or anything. You can make time for everything only if you master balance in your life.

I'll tell you about the eight pillars, that you can find everywhere if you dig deep and search, for a meaningful balanced life. All I'm trying to do is make it easier for you to know about them. After doing my research, I realized that a lot of us don't know about basic stuff that we should know about and that they are out there waiting for us to discover them or know they exist.

The eight pillars of a balanced life are:

1. Physical wellness
2. Mental wellness
3. Emotionalwellness
4. Spiritualwellness
5. Socialwellness
6. Environmentalwellness

7. Financialwellness

8. Occupationalwellness

Physical wellness

Physical wellness is the key component to your overall wellness. Because without physical health, we cannot enjoy anything in this world. It all will not make sense to us anymore. When you are sick, you don't care which party you will miss today or what car you want to ride. Your body is in pain and all you think about is to get back on your feet and stop this pain, that's your only target. On the contrary, you will think clearer when you are in good health and less stressed.

When you have physical wellness, you should be so grateful and take more care of your body. Do more exercise, sleep properly, and eat healthily. Sleep not less than 7 hours daily. Eat well and eat healthy food. Drink a lot of water. If you like yoga, practice it often because it's very healthy for your body and mind.

Mental wellness

Mental health is about having a positive mindset. It's the golden mind that buys you happiness at its lowest price because you master how to live happily and be positive in life.

You can use some tips to train your mind to be in a positive mood always. Start by meditating and relaxing your body and mind for a few minutes every day. Visualize the most beautiful things you want, as applied with the law of attraction, to attract the best for you and make your mind feel that you own what you want, so it becomes more positive.

Reconstruct your thoughts, and get out all your feelings, the positive and the negative. Save your energy for the best things, and if needed deactivate from social media and social life for a while. Always do what is better for you and makes you grow.

Another kind of mental wellness is intellectual wellness; it is the next step after having a positive mindset to work on making it grow in the right direction.

Intellectual wellness is having a learner's mindset, always wanting to know more and do more. It makes you move from one place to another.

There is a sentence that I love a lot, "if you're the smartest person in the room, you're in the wrong room". Always be around people who challenge your mind to a new level.

Emotional wellness

Our feelings are us, they are very important, they affect every aspect of our life, and they can motivate us to the top or drag us down to the bottom. They affect our behavior, actions, and motivation. So, let's take care of our feelings and not ignore them or force them out. You have to understand your feelings and let yourself express them without judging yourself for what you feel. Try to understand them.

The following are some tips you could use to shift your mood and have emotional wellness:

First of all, allow yourself to feel whatever you are feeling. Express your feelings and never judge yourself. Also, meditation and yoga might always be an idea to clear your mind and make you feel good. You can also listen to music; music can shift your mood sometimes. Write if you like it, or paint, or dance. Express yourself and your feelings through any kind of art or hobby you like.

Then, manage your stress level with self-care, it's good to take good care of yourself, and it helps you to have a well-balanced mood. Practice deep breathing too.

Last, ask for help if you feel you need it and if things are more than you could handle.

Spiritual wellness

It is living by your set of morals and values, finding inner peace, and living each day to the fullest with mindfulness and happiness. It is to be aware and present to the maximum and live in this moment and make what makes you happy now. It is to be grateful for the things you already have, it's good and spiritual to practice gratitude. Connect with the higher power and pray. Connect with nature, trees, and land. Feel nature through your inhalation and exhalation. Take time for self-reflection, take time for yourself, go out with yourself, take care of yourself, and connect with it and know "you" more. You are the greatest discovery.

Social wellness

People are important in your life no matter how much you feel you don't want to be close to them. You can't live alone. You have to feel such things as being respected, accepted, and safe.

To be connected with others and have healthy relationships, surround yourself with good and supportive people. You have to be part of the positive community, spend time with your loved ones, and be there for helping them. Be useful, help others, and serve them if needed. Hear thank you from someone you love. Teach people something you know or it won't have any value if you don't share it and make others benefit from it. *Important information is only important when it helps others, then it's important.* Communicating with people around you is so important; it makes you transform your feelings and makes you alive when interacting with another important human being in your life.

Environmental wellness

Environmental involves your environment and respecting the environment around you. It has a direct impact on your mindset, creativity, and productivity like water, earth, and air. The place where you sit, sleep or work has a direct influence on you. So, keep it clean and fresh. Clean your room, drawers, and house. Put some flowers and design the place where you sit. Always keep your environment light and clean and this will have a positive effect on your mental and emotional health.

Financial wellness

It's your relationship with money. It's how to manage financial expenses, how to save some money or a lot of it, and how to make money. The most important is to have the confidence that you can absorb a financial shock. So, you could live with peace of mind and not worry all the time about what you have to do.

However, this pillar stresses people a lot so it's important to know how to manage your life in this area of life. So, take time to plan and budget, get rid of excess debt, save some money as an emergency fund, and invest and build assets

Occupational wellness

It's career satisfaction. It's to feel that what you're doing is meaningful. Occupational wellness is about finding purpose and meaning in what you're doing, not just doing it for someone else. It's something you love from the core. That is the thing that I was trying to find in you from the beginning of Chapter One. A lot of people don't know it. They act just to act and work just to work. I'm sure if you start without knowing it, you now know about it or already you have started searching for it. It's not hard to find, it's in you.

All those eight pillars are important to have in your life or have a little of each of them so you can balance your life. Also, you will have goals and take care of your finances, and you will know the importance of your social life and your spiritual life on the other hand. You will know when to be alone and when you need to be with your beloved ones. Your health, body, and mental health need to be taken care of. Your emotions are not less important than any of the above. You need the eight pillars to balance your life accordingly. They are all connected.

Balance is the key to true happiness. When you balance, you don't get lost on your way. You don't miss "you" in some areas of life. You don't miss the fun because you are a workaholic, and you don't feel useless because you're always partying. You don't miss having someone in your life because you are so introverted and always alone, and you don't get mad and miss yourself because you are always too loud and with people.

You always find yourself in every aspect of your life because you're always there. So, master the art of balance and get your right pill of it at the right moment.

The phase when it is all on track

This is when you know who are you and what you want from this life.

Do you want to be a doctor? Then go and be a doctor. Do you want to be a lawyer? You can be that. If you want to become a singer, go for it. If you want to be a million things, go and be a million things. Even if you don't want to be anything, don't.

All you have to do is to ask yourself this one single question:

What makes me happy?

It's not easy to reach your aims.You have to give it a lot of time and work on yourself, but who the hell said you cannot be the person you want to become?

You can do it all and you can start here and now. Don't make excuses. I already did that before you and don't say I'm not ready because there's no right time to be ready. Just start from somewhere, anywhere and everything will lead.

Get moving, go search for what you want, fail in it thousands of times, and you'll reach it in the end.No matter how hard and bumpy the road is, you will get there before you even realize it.

Do you know why? Because you have that desire. The desire and the passion for a thing that you want, and that you will give anything to have. The most important thing is not just how to do it but how to do it in your unique way. There's no such thing called right, there's a thing called how you feel about it and how your passion will drive you to do it.

It might not be right, but it'll reach a lot more people when it's unique and different and from your heart. So, your power here is you. Only you.

You are the master of your destiny. You should have faith in yourself.

And faith in God. God is the existence that I most believe in because he had always been there for me. He's always here, pray for him and ask him for what you want. Believe it deep inside that there is nothing bigger than the one who created us from nothing. Think about our cells and every tiny little thing in our body, and how it works as a super machine with a system no one can ever create. Believe that there is someone bigger than every situation and that he can solve every problem no matter how big it might seem to you. It's very easy for God who created the night, the day, the stars, the planets, the sea, the rivers, and all the creatures in this world. But there you are still sitting sadly on your couch thinking that there is something bigger than you that can't be solved.

Pray to him in your language, ask him what you want, and visualize that he gave it to you. Believe in the good of

God and he won't let you down. Even when he delays something for you, it's for your good, believe me. It happened to me a lot and I knew it later. Just ask him and let him be your mentor, he's always around you. Feel him. Pray for him in every single thing you do or you want to do. Always have faith that he's with you in your journey.

Start your day by saying I believe in you God and I believe in myself, I'll try to do my best today and I'll leave it all in your hands. Be kind to me and give me what I want. Talk positively to yourself and be kind to it too.

You work hard through those pages trying to figure out who you are, what you want to become, and how to get rid of beliefs and manners that block your way and hold you back away from the success and happy life that you deserve to have.

So, it's time. Now is the right time.

Life is like a dream, it begins one day and ends another day. You live it all like a dream. Live it happily because anyway it's going to end soon and very soon…

The day that you don't fear death is the day when you're truly living and enjoying this life because you don't fear unfinished purposes, you don't fear going without knowing why you came. You know now why you came to this life and you are living up to it. But you always fear when you're still not done. It's never time for you to leave as it wasn't time for you to move and discover who you are and work on it. So either way it's too late. So don't be one of the people that I call "the lifetime regretters"

In the end, I want to tell you to be so proud of yourself because at least you are trying to discover yourself even if you think you are far away from a happy, successful, and balanced life. You will be there when you realize it and be aware of yourself. Realizing what's going on in you is the first and best cure for you. Keep it up, and always be proud of how far you've come.

Success is not in one aspect of life, it's a journey of happy days and moments through every aspect of your life, it's a package of you with your qualities within. In your life stages, in every part of your life, in your career, family, friends, habits, confidence, in letting go of what doesn't serve you, in thinking positively and attracting good things, always understand your weakness and fears, realize your uniqueness, and don't envy others. Trust yourself and God. Be disciplined, work hard for your aims, and worry just about what matters the most. Balance and organize your life. The most important thing is to love yourself and you'll be there.

Just always remember to be happy through the journey, and to feel that your journey is worth living.

Don't ever forget that a successful person is a happy one.

And you deserve to be the one.

Sincerely,

With love